WITHDRAWN

Rolando Hinojosa
and the American Dream

Rolando Hinojosa
and the
American Dream

Texas Writers Series

by Joyce Glover Lee

University of North Texas Press
Denton, Texas

TEXAS WRITERS SERIES NUMBER 5
General Editor James Ward Lee

Permissions:
University of North Texas Press
PO Box 311336
Denton TX 76203-1336

First printed in 1997 in the United States of America

5   4   3   2   1

The paper in this book meets the minimum requirements of
the American National Standard for Permanence of Paper for
Printed Library Materials, Z39.48-1984.

Library of Congress Cataloging-in-Publication Data

Lee, Joyce Glover, 1954-
Rolando Hinojosa and the American dream / Joyce Glover Lee.
        p.   cm. — (Texas writers series : no. 5)
Includes bibliographical references (p.) and index.
ISBN 1-57441-023-7 (cloth : alk. paper)
1. Hinojosa, Rolando—Criticism and interpretation. 2. Mexican
Americans in literature. 3. Success in literature. 4. Texas—
In literature. 5. Myth in literature. I. Title. II. Series.
                PS3558.I545Z76   1997
        813'.54—dc21   96-50027
                                        CIP

Dedication

In Memoriam
Gordon Louis Glover
1921-1995

Table of Contents

Acknowledgments

Many good friends came to my aid while I was preparing this manuscript for publication. Their practical assistance and emotional support made my work easier, and I am in their debt. In particular, I wish to thank Giles R. Mitchell, J. F. Kobler, and James T. F. Tanner of the UNT Department of English for their advice and their interest in this project. Don Graham of the University of Texas at Austin gave me invaluable help by reading and criticizing the final manuscript, helping me to make it a better work than it would have been otherwise. I would also like to thank James W. Lee for his help and consideration.

1

American Odyssey

Despite the fact that most of the criticism of Rolando Hinojosa's *Klail City Death Trip Series*[1] may be termed "Chicano criticism," and despite the fact that much of this criticism offers significant insight into the *Death Trip*, two equally significant facts are that this body of criticism tends toward repetition, as it builds a fence around Hinojosa's work, claiming it primarily for a Chicano audience.[2] It is my hope to knock a few gaps in that fence. I intend to look at Hinojosa's *Death Trip Series* from what I see as a broader perspective and to place Hinojosa's work within the larger canon of that vague, elusive body that we call "American literature." In doing so, I do not intend to deny or to ignore Hinojosa's

Mexican-American subject matter or his regional ori-
entation, but simply to consider them as elements of
a larger construct.[3] The nine books that make up the
Death Trip Series fit the definitions of the "sequence
novel," a well-understood but still largely undefined
group of novels treating a single set of characters or
a single place or theme developed through the generations of a specific locale. Hardy's "Wessex novels,"
Trollope's "Barset novels," Anthony Powell's *A Dance
to the Music of Time*, and Faulkner's rather looser
series, the "Yoknapatawpha novels," are examples.
The sequence novel, or to use the French term, the
roman fleuve, allows an author greater range than a
single novel, and it is this extended range that helps
to take Hinojosa's novels and poems outside the con-
fines of the Río Grande Valley and into the broad
stream of American literature.

As I see it, to give Hinojosa his due, not just as a
"Mexican-American" writer or "Chicano" writer, or
even as a "Texas" writer, but instead as an American
writer, one must first consider the *Death Trip Series*
as a work that falls primarily into the category of
American fiction. Hinojosa, after all, is as much an
American as he is a Texan, Texas Mexican, Mexican
American, Chicano, etc. At the same time, it is not
possible to be insensible to Hinojosa's regionalism or
his work's distinct place in regional American literature. Certainly Hinojosa is a "Texas writer," and his

sense of place is centered in the Texas Valley, a world in itself and a place recognizable by all Texans as a discrete community, far removed from the Piney Woods, the Llano Estacado, or the urban giants of Dallas and Houston. Yet, though we give Hinojosa this very specific designation—chronicler of the Valley—and despite those limited geographical parameters, it is both unfair and unenlightening to treat him as a "small" writer whose compass is limited to a tiny segment of America. His *Death Trip Series* should be read as we read the work of any American regionalist, for Hinojosa's work transcends the regional, transcends the Valley, transcends Texas, while it remains rooted in all three.

An objective reader of the *Klail City Death Trip Series* cannot fail to perceive the variations played on the American dream of success and acculturation, nor can an informed reader fail to perceive the parallels between Hinojosa's own life and the lives that appear in the *Death Trip*. Most of Hinojosa's major characters, particularly Rafe Buenrostro and Jehú Malacara, are essentially his own age and their lives mimic his own in a remarkable manner. As children, these characters, like Hinojosa, live primarily in the "Mexican" community of their small towns. Later, they attend integrated schools and American universities, serve in the military, teach school, or enter into business. All make some spoken or unspoken decision to succeed—in the conventional American sense of the word—within the Anglo community. As Sandra Cisnéros has said of Mexican-American writers,

> We're writers, but we're coming from homes where there were no books and the radio was on. We're the first generation to get up and write a book. That makes the kind of stories and issues we write about very different, say, from the García Márquezes or the Laura Esquivels. In stories their families were families with servants. We are the servants. We don't write magical realism. Our issues are grounded in working class issues. (*Austin American-Statesman*, 17 September 1993, C1)

Hinojosa's experience is essentially the same as Cisnéros's, and the successes of Rafe Buenrostro and Jehú Malacara mirror the success of Rolando Hinojosa. As Hinojosa moved away from the world of the *barrio mexicano* to take his place in academic and literary society, so Rafe and Jehú begin to reach beyond the barrio background and grasp the American Dream. It is precisely these connections between author and protagonists that force Hinojosa to confront in his fiction the pervasiveness of American myth with all its attendant ironies and contradictions.

Hinojosa's characters, like Hinojosa himself, have a sense of the past. And within the world of the *Death Trip Series* the very word "past" is imbued with romance, glory, and, more important, *possibility*: possibility lost, unlikely to be regained. "Past" fuses nostalgia and melancholy with, ironically, a desperate need to *act*, to *be* in some way. However, the present-day acting and being may be seen as inferior to the old ways, to the possibilities that were inherent in the past. So, along with any number of American heroes before them, Hinojosa's major characters are driven to propel themselves forward at the same time that they look backward with sadness and regret. As Ramón Saldívar has noted, Rafe and Jehú are "Janus-like" characters (*Chicano Narrative* 136) with the ability to look in two directions at once. There is at once a new pragmatism and a new romanticism at work; these characters are compelled to seek a new route, but in doing so, anything and everything may be just beyond the next bend in the road—and anything and everything may call back the paradise lost.

Hinojosa's characters, like many others before them, are engaged in the ultimate quest: the quest for a new life. Once this fact is firmly established, the *Death Trip Series* cannot go anywhere but forward. And once the trip has begun, it becomes a true American odyssey.[4] In fact, though I will argue that it is structured as a sequence novel, the *Death Trip* may also be read as a type of epic poem, for the journey made by Rafe Buenrostro and Jehú Malacara is beset by one danger after another, some of them the actual physical dangers of deprivation and war, many of them emotional coils in which Rafe and Jehú appear trapped by birth and circumstance. Yet they not only overcome; they prevail. And it is their ultimate triumph that reassures us—if at times we question what seems to be a naively benign conclusion to such a difficult journey—that although order may descend into chaos, surely order will gain ascendancy. We suspend our disbelief somewhat reluctantly because we know that racial intolerance, institutionalized racism, and outright contempt for ethnic minorities is widespread. We also understand the formidable barriers of language and economic circumstances. Yet Hinojosa manages to convince us on some level that though the American Dream may be gasping for air, it has not yet expired.

In the epigraph to *The Valley*, Hinojosa quotes Matthew Arnold's famous lines from "Stanzas from the Grand Chartreuse": "Born between two worlds, one dead and one as yet unborn" (though somewhat altered from Arnold's "Wandering between two worlds, one dead/The other powerless to be born"). This is an apt epigraph for the first novel in a sequence entitled the *Klail City Death Trip Series*, for the world that Rafe, Jehú, and others will move into *is* as yet unborn (for them) in the 1930s and 40s. Yet the possibility—perhaps the inevitability—of its birth is certain. By the 70s and 80s, that world seems to have been birthed, but the arrival of this new life has signaled the death of the old one in the process. Hinojosa chronicles the long struggle, the birth and death pangs, during the years in between.

As the chronicle unfolds, several manifestations of American mythology arise. The theme that since Cooper's *Leatherstocking Tales* has dominated so much of American literature emerges: the question of community versus individuality. In Hinojosa's fiction, this question is enlarged and complicated by the idea of "progress" and affluence. Cooper's Leatherstocking, a radical representation of Cooper's own fear that the Jeffersonian ideal would be corrupted by commercialization, is perhaps our first truly American hero, and he chooses separateness. He presses westward, seeking freedom from the pressures of society and those who espouse progress and affluence, just as Huck Finn does almost a hundred years later. But even in Cooper's day, escape is problematical. At the same time that Leatherstocking probes the western edges of the frontier, a great mass of westering pioneers follows close upon his heels, not treading lightly, but seeking to exploit whatever material riches the land may have to offer. To Cooper's dismay, most settlers of the North American continent sought an *el*

Dorado rather than a democratic community based on moral worth.

In any case, by the time Hinojosa introduces his twentieth-century heroes, the original dream has been so completely perverted that a Leatherstocking—or a Huck Finn—cannot exist even in the imagination. In our own time, we must resort to the movie version of, say, an "E.T.," an extraterrestrial, to enable us to conceive of anything like the radical purity of a Leatherstocking or a Huck Finn. Hinojosa's characters, unlike the hero of the film *E.T.*, are rooted firmly in a recognizable time and place. They are merely human and they are intractably caught up in an ironic inversion of the American myth of the westering pioneer. As Edwin T. Bowden observes, "The world of the old frontier is gone, and with it the Huck Finns and the Deerslayers" (64). The frontier motif did not die, though; it just moved west, underwent a few permutations, and finally, at the present state of American history and culture, is still sufficiently vital to appear in a "marginal" literary work such as the *Klail City Death Trip Series*. Rafe and Jehú perceive, as the Eagles' song declares, "there is no new frontier; we have got to make it here."

Unlike traditional characters in American literature—and myth—who go forth to face and conquer a natural wilderness, Hinojosa's characters find their wilderness in the Anglo culture that has dominated the Valley since early in this century. They do not decide or choose to face this wilderness; as Mexican Americans in a dominant Anglo world, they are born into conflict, and the challenge is imposed upon them. Though they differ in some ways from the traditional "seekers" in American literature, Hinojosa's characters also share similarities with those earlier pilgrims. Hinojosa's main characters have to find stronger weapons than "a rifle, an axe, and hoe" in order to enter and subdue the wilderness, but they are able to do so because, like their literary predecessors, they are exceptional in one way or another, particularly in their ability to endure (Karolides 14, 42, 247). Failure to confront the challenge, failure to win the battle, means more than just maintaining the *status quo*: it means that they become nonentities. They are not players, they are not even on the field. They can take no meaningful part in the larger culture.

Traditionally, the westering pioneer often had an "old home" or even an "old world" which was more or less intact and to which he might repair if the road west proved too rocky or the promised land less than paradise. Hinojosa's characters have instead a fragmenting community, a world of chasms and abysses, a world of change. As Hinojosa says, suggesting the lack of choice the Mexican American has in this matter, "whether the Texas-Mexican admits it or not, he is greatly influenced by this *overwhelming* [italics

mine] culture and economy" (qtd. in José David
Saldívar, "Our Southwest" 184).

Hinojosa's use of the word "economy" is revealing, for it is the commercial culture of the Anglo world
that must be successfully negotiated if other nego-
tiations are to occur. What Cooper, Jefferson, and others feared has come to pass. American culture and
society are based upon economic rather than truly
democratic constructs. We cannot easily imagine
Jefferson's ideal community. And, as much as anything else, Hinojosa's characters are caught up in the
quest to attain the American Dream in the most conventional sense of that term: the good life, the afflu-
ent, materially comfortable life. But that life may have
to be purchased at the cost of a satisfying spiritual or
internal life.

The search for the good life that we see in the
Death Trip, at its present state of completion, endorses
educational and material advantage over ethnic ho-
mogeneity. Denis Donoghue calls this outlook
"Franklinism" (12), arguing that as one operates under this "ism," he also experiences a "deep self-criti-
cism for the part that goes along willingly enough
with acquisition and greed" (8). Rafe and Jehú cannot be accused of greed, but they, as well as many of
the other characters, do enter into the Anglo world
which exhorts one to "get ahead" and to "make good,"
no matter what the cost to one's spirit. Throughout

much of the *Series*, however, Rafe and Jehú's ambivalence about and detachment from Anglo life and Anglo
institutions reveal that at the very least they undergo
a kind of soul-searching as they move from the old
world to the new.

Yet Hinojosa fails to document the depths of this
experience adequately. That his heroes feel ambiva-
lent about this "trip" they are on is inevitable; not
only are they moving from one place and time to a
different place and time, they are also moving into a
form of isolation, paradoxically, just as they are moving into the larger society. Their isolation is not the
traditional isolation of the lone figure on the frontier,
but a psychic isolation from old ways and old memories, a conscious setting aside of a part of the self.
Ramón Saldívar, writing of the Mexican-American
folk ballad, the *corrido*, and its hero, says it

> depicts a common working man put into an
> uncommon situation by the power of cultural
> and historical forces beyond his control. . . .
> the corrido's hero's individual life sequences
> have not yet become totally distinct from
> those of his community. (*"Korean Love Songs"*
> 136)

Hinojosa's main characters differ from the hero of the
corrido in that they are not "common men," they are

exceptional—Hinojosa refers to Jehú as the "uncommon banker," and reveals Rafe's superior character through his wartime journal. Rafe and Jehú do find themselves in some "uncommon situations" over which they have little or no control. But they differ again from the hero of the *corrido* in that as time passes, their life experiences become more clearly individual rather than communal. Because of this movement away from the communal culture, Rafe and Jehú necessarily experience a sense of loss.

Edwin T. Bowden notes that while isolation was for Deerslayer "a state to be sought," it is also likely that "such a man and such a state never were" (64). His argument is that Deerslayer represents an ideal, not an actuality, and that for human beings—or their fictional representatives—isolation cannot be forever endured. Rafe and Jehú cannot thrive in a state of isolation, and forces beyond their control compel them to "connect" in one way or another with the powerful Anglo world. They learn how to win in the Anglo world, though they occasionally seem like some of Henry James's young heroines who, in their efforts to find husbands, are engaged in a similar quest: "Generally, James has his girls defeat [their] men at their own dreadful game, especially if the men are Europeans far gone in corruption, but the victorious girls are left wondering just what it is they have won" (Donoghue 115). Hinojosa's Mexican Americans are often just as troubled as James's young women, for to shrink from conflict challenges their identity as Americans, yet the very attempt to win, not to mention actual success, actual winning, necessitates some sort of denial of the ethnic self. Hinojosa uses this dilemma and all its ramifications as one of the bases for his work. The unrelenting fact of their ethnicity is central to all his major characters because it is the main stumbling block in their quest for social and economic parity with the Anglos, but it is also their center, their rootedness. So the conflict of the *Klail City Death Trip Series* is both external and internal, personal and public, and one cannot be separated from the other. Hinojosa's essays and speeches, as well as the works that constitute the *Death Trip* itself, reveal his understanding of this difficult fact.

The search for the American Dream that Hinojosa explores falls into three definite chronological periods. The first of these is the 1930s (*The Valley*, *Klail City*, and parts of *Claros Varones de Belken*), when the Texas Mexican community seems insular, isolated from the Anglo community, and his two main characters, Rafe Buenrostro and Jehú Malacara, are young boys. In the novels that look back to the thirties, an air of nostalgia permeates the action. Perhaps this looking backward is not surprising since many of the characters are essentially nineteenth-century figures—old-time patriarchs and matriarchs, veterans of the Mexican Revolution, and other Valleyites who remember the romance of war and a life devoted to a cause. In addition, because of the insularity of the Mexican community, people depend upon one another in a vital way. For example, when Jehú is orphaned, he ends up traveling quite happily with don Victor Peláez, working in the carnival owned by don Victor's brother. There is no suggestion of outside—Anglo governmental—interference, and Jehú's relatives are apparently happy to have Jehú cared for by such a friend, even though don Victor is not related to the family.

The second chronological period occurs after World War II, when change is more evident in the Valley, and Jehú and Rafe are in their young manhood. In *Korean Love Songs*, *The Useless Servants*, *Rites and Witnesses*, *Dear Rafe*, and parts of *Claros Varones de Belken* one sees very clearly the intrusion of the Anglo world and Anglo concerns. One might say that as Rafe and Jehú move into adulthood, they must move out of the comfortable world of Mexican culture and begin to face up to Anglo culture in almost every aspect of life. But the transition from *mejicano* to Mexican American is slow. When Jehú attends a fundraising barbecue for a Mexican-American political candidate at his Anglo employer's house, a local Anglo woman seated near him delivers a loud monologue on "Mexicans."

In *Partners in Crime* and *Becky and Her Friends*, which move into the 1970s, the Valley Mexican appears to have come into his own. Jehú and Rafe are successful (one in banking, the other in law enforcement) within the still dominant but less powerful Anglo establishment. In *Becky*, Hinojosa treats the subject of the professional Mexican-American woman in the character of Becky Escobar. With her liberation and the growth and maturation of Jehú and Rafe, Hinojosa attempts to reveal how the assumptions of the Texas Mexican community and race relations have changed from the 1930s to the present.

The author's life closely mirrors the movement of the sequence. Rolando Hinojosa (his name appears as Rolando Hinojosa-Smith on some of his earlier works) was born Romeo Rolando Hinojosa in Mercedes, Texas, in 1929, a product of both the Texas Mexican and Texas Anglo cultures. His mother, an Anglo, was a descendant of settlers who came to the Valley in 1887, a generation before the Missouri Pacific Railroad came there in 1904 and opened it to great numbers of Anglo farmers and businessmen. Hinojosa's father was descended from the Spanish colonists who came in the eighteenth century to one of New Spain's northern provinces, Nuevo Santander, which lay along both sides of the Río Grande River.

As a boy, Hinojosa was educated in both Mexican and American schools in Mercedes and became equally at home with Spanish and English. After being graduated from Mercedes High School, Hinojosa entered the army and was promoted to the rank of sergeant before he finished his term of service and enrolled in the University of Texas at Austin. The Korean War interrupted his studies, and he served in combat in Korea as a lieutenant before returning to Austin to complete his degree in Spanish in 1953.

From 1953 to 1956, and again from 1959 to 1961, Hinojosa taught Spanish, history, and government at Brownsville High School, but between 1956 and 1961, he worked for a chemical company and did a stint with the U. S. Civil Service Commission. In 1961, he entered New Mexico Highlands University and took a master's degree in Spanish in 1962. He then began work toward a Ph.D. in Spanish at the University of Illinois, graduating in 1969. His first university job was in the Foreign Language Department at Trinity University in San Antonio, where he taught from 1968 to 1970. Leaving Trinity, Hinojosa spent the next seven years at Texas A&I University in Kingsville, where he served variously as Chairman of Modern Languages, Dean of Arts and Sciences, and Vice President for Academic Affairs.

After winning the Premio Quinto Sol for his first novel, *Estampas del valle y otras obras* (1973), and the prestigious South American Premio Casa de las Américas for his second, *Klail City y sus alrededores*

(1976), he was cited as having produced the "Best Writing in the Humanities" by the Southwest Conference on Latin American Studies in 1982. In 1977, Hinojosa accepted a post as Director of Chicano Studies and Professor of English at the University of Minnesota. He remained in Minnesota until 1981, when he accepted a position as Professor of English at the University of Texas at Austin. He now holds the Ellen Clayton Garwood Professorship in Creative Writing at the University of Texas.

Though Hinojosa has left the Valley, it remains his spiritual home. In a sense the Texas Valley symbolizes for Hinojosa what the concept of Aztlán symbolizes for more radical Chicano writers, though perhaps a better way to clarify Hinojosa's view of the Valley is to compare it to James Joyce's view of Ireland.[5] Like Joyce, Hinojosa is an exile from his homeland. He had to leave the Valley—and then write about it as he remembered it—in order to understand it and come to terms with it. Hinojosa's fiction resembles Joyce's in several ways, most notably in structure and in the use of autobiography. In addition, what Harry Levin says of Joyce's fiction applies as well to Hinojosa's: Levin says the writing "is not an act of creation but an act of evocation peculiarly saturated with reminiscences" (qtd. in Morris, "The Territory Ahead" 343). Like Joyce's Ireland, Hinojosa's Valley is home to a strong culture with a turbulent history, a history of domination and resistance. Often the major landholders—and thus the powerbrokers—are "outsiders." Also, as in Ireland, the "native" culture of the Valley is Catholic, the outsider culture, Protestant. But deeper than these obvious parallels is the love/hate relationship that both Joyce and Hinojosa experience with their homelands. Joyce's essential ambivalence toward Ireland is well-documented, and Hinojosa asserts that the Valley is both "reviled and beloved" (*Claros Varones de Belken* 208).

Hinojosa's observations not only of the folk culture but also of the political machinery of his fictional Belken County reveal his ambivalence toward the entire system as well as his understanding of it. The Klail City Bank, for example, holds the power in Belken County, though those who wield the power are a degenerate lot compared to Colonel Klail, the founder of the family in South Texas. Hinojosa clearly took the famous Texas King Ranch as a model for his KBC Ranch and its extended holdings—including the bank. Even though the King Ranch is not in the Valley proper, the kind of influence exerted by the King-Kleberg family and the King Ranch Corporation was well-known throughout the small communities of the Valley. (And there is no question that Hinojosa's years at Texas A&I in Kingsville provided him with a closer look at the influence the King Ranch had on a large portion of South Texas.) These Anglo outsiders corrupt the vision of the Valley-as-it-was in a glorious past. Yet Hinojosa also shows that the glorious past— before the infiltration of the Anglo—was not untroubled by greed, ignorance, and political manipulation. Like Joyce, Hinojosa casts a loving if sometimes disapproving eye on his homeland. He is obsessed by it in all its manifestations.

That the place we know as the Texas Valley should command such attention is hardly remarkable, for it has had a long and varied history. Its sheer vividness as a geographical region lends it sufficient interest as a literary setting, but it is the history and culture of the various peoples who have inhabited it that appeal to the writer's imagination. The early European movement into what is often called Spanish Texas began in the sixteenth century with expeditions led by Cabeza de Vaca and Coronado. As Donald Chipman has noted, "Spanish settlement in Texas . . . was planned by the King and his agents, usually with the intent of achieving specific military, political, and spiritual objectives" (8). But these objectives were rarely, or only temporarily, met. The remoteness of Spanish Texas made its problems less significant to the Spanish bureaucracy in Madrid than the troubles between Mexico City and Spain. "Indian problems" constituted a major part of the frontier experience for at least two hundred years, by which time Anglo settlers were crossing, legally and illegally, into Spanish Texas.

Though Spain attempted to keep out "land-hungry Anglo-Americans," Chipman argues that Spain's goal of keeping Spanish America safe from outsiders was doomed by a series of European events: "the ambitions of Napoleon Bonaparte, revolution in the heartland of New Spain, and the reactionary policies of King Ferdinand VII in Spain itself" (Chipman 216). By the summer of 1821, when Mexico successfully rebelled against Spanish domination, "Texas passed from Spanish to Mexican control with scarcely a protest by its inhabitants" (Chipman 240).

The Anglo influence grew dramatically with the advent of Mexican independence. For example, "a changed attitude of support for the border towns' American trading links was opened up with Mexican independence in 1821" (Kearney 35), and furthered as U. S. and Mexican rail systems were connected. The resulting increase in business had a significant impact on Border culture: "The American towns took the initiative in launching farms. An urgent need for quantities of farm workers was met by workers from the Mexican side of the border" (Kearney 122). This fact, along with the Tejanos' loss of their lands—often lucrative ranches—by means often more foul than fair, and the brutality of the Texas Rangers set up much of the racial conflict that persists in some form to this day. In addition, the political situation which prevailed well into this century engendered discord within the Mexican-American community itself and helped to institutionalize the paternalistic system that was already in place in most of the border towns. Texas politics, firmly in the hands of "the conservative wing of the Democratic Party in the tradition of the post-Reconstruction South. . . . penetrated down to the local level" (Kearney 209).

El Paso offers a typical example of the grip party politics had on the Texas-Mexican border. In 1889, the Democratic Party controlled El Paso by means of "the Ring," which "utilized all the borderland techniques for manipulating the Mexican vote, including paying voters, paying poll taxes, and 'corralling' voters overnight in order to ensure their vote on election day." The more assimilated a Mexican American, the better his chances of being a part of the Ring and being used as a kind of liaison between the Anglo and the Mexican-American community (Kearney 187–88). This "assimilated" Mexican American oftentimes gave the idea of assimilation or acculturation a bad name as far as the Mexican-American community was concerned.

As the twentieth century wore on, as world wars had their effect even on such a remote, rural place as the Texas Valley, as the civil rights movement began to grow, the world Rolando Hinojosa writes of became

even more varied. For all these reasons and more,
Hinojosa found himself with ample material out of
which to create a portrait of a place, a people, and a
time which are a quintessential part of the American
experience.

The world of the Texas Valley that Rolando
Hinojosa has created began appearing in stories,
tales, sketches, and finally novels (first in Spanish,
then in translations, and later in English). The nature of their publication makes the chronology of
Hinojosa's novels and stories hard to trace. Gaps between the time a work was written and its publication, reprintings, retranslations, and the variety of
titles for essentially the same material all confound
the newcomer to the *Klail City Death Trip Series*. The
first novel, *Estampas del Valle y otras obras*, for example, was written in Spanish, translated by Gustavo
Valadez and José Reyna. It appeared in a Spanish/
English edition published by Editorial Justa Publications in 1973. In 1983, Hinojosa recreated the novel
in English, and it was published as *The Valley* by Bilingual Press/Editorial Bilingüe.

Perhaps none of his books has seen more permutations than his second novel, also written in Spanish, which won the Casa de las Americas prize for
fiction in 1976. Hinojosa called the book *Notas,
Generaciones y Brechas*. The manuscript was translated into English by Rosaura Sánchez and published

by Justa Publications in 1977 under the title *Generaciones y semblanzas*. Another edition appeared in 1978 with additional material and a different translator, Fausto Avedano, under the title *Generaciones, Notas y Brechas*. Then in 1987, Hinojosa rewrote the book in English under the title *Klail City*, published by Arte Público Press of Houston.

Next Hinojosa wrote, again in English, the book of poems *Korean Love Songs* (1978). It was published by Editorial Justa. In 1979–80, he wrote *Claros Varones de Belken* in Spanish, but it was not published until 1986, after Bilingual Press/Editorial Bilingüe had Julia Cruz translate it into English.

In 1981, *Mi querido Rafa* was published by Arte Público. Hinojosa rewrote it in English as *Dear Rafe*, and, in 1985, Arte Público released the new edition. In 1982, *Rites and Witnesses: A Comedy* was published by Arte Público. It is in English, as are the last three novels in the series, *Partners in Crime* (Arte Público 1985), *Becky and Her Friends* (Arte Público 1990), and *The Useless Servants* (Arte Público 1993), set in Korea and complementing the material found in *Korean Love Songs*.

This rather strange publishing history and the multiplicity of titles make it seem that the *Klail City Death Trip Series* comprises a large body of work. However, taken together, the novels that make up the *Series* run to approximately a thousand pages. If

one were to subtract the number of pages that are
repetitions—the same events are often recounted in
two or three or even more of the books—the total
number of pages shrinks significantly.

The repetition of events and the dates of publication prevent me from analyzing these works individually or in chronological order.[6] Such an analysis would
also be repetitious and it seems to me practically useless. I have chosen instead to examine the series the-
matically and structurally, while trying to preserve
some sense of its historical chronology. In doing so, I
hope to give Hinojosa his due, not only as a regional
writer, but also as an American writer, because I believe that in the *Klail City Death Trip Series* Rolando
Hinojosa captures an American experience which is
both culturally enlightening and spiritually enrich-
ing.

---

[1] Hinojosa himself, and scholars and critics of his work, refer
to his works collectively as the *Klail City Death Trip Series*. The
researcher should be aware, however, that it is not a traditional
series (i.e., a planned sequence of publications by a single publisher), and will not have a series title listing in library catalogs,
online or otherwise. For the purposes of this book, however, the
author conforms to common usage and refers to the books as the
Klail City Death Trip Series.

[2] The best recent Chicano criticism can be found in José David Saldívar's "Chicano Border Narratives as Cultural Critique," in *Criticism in the Borderlands: Studies in Chicano Literature, Culture, and Ideology* (Héctor Calderón and J. D. Saldívar, eds.), and in his *The Dialectics of Our America: Genealogy, Cultural Critique, and Literary History*. See also Ramón Saldívar's *Chicano Narrative: The Dialectics of Difference*, and Wilson Neate's "The Function of Belken County in the Fiction of Rolando Hinojosa: The Voicing of the Chicano Experience" in *American Review: A Review of Hispanic Literature and Art of the USA*.

[3] Two recent dissertations deal with Hinojosa's role in the American literary canon and as an ethnic regionalist. See Jaime Armin Mejía's dissertation, "Transformations in Rolando Hinojosa's *Klail City Death Trip Series*." See also Laurence Lee McClain's dissertation, "The Rhetoric of Regional Identity: The Politics of American Literary History" and Manuel Martín-Rodríguez's 1991 dissertation, "*Klail City Death Trip* de Rolando Hinojosa: La novela del lector" for a reader-response theory and speech-act theory analysis.

[4] Héctor Calderón in "Texas Border Literature: Cultural Transformations and Historical Reflections in the Works of Américo Paredes, Rolando Hinojosa, and Gloria Anzaldúa" notes "obvious points of contact with Spanish historiography from the period of transition between the Medieval Age and the Renaissance, with the works *Generaziones y semblanzas* (1450) by Fernán Pérez de Guzmán and *Claros varones de Castilla* (1489) by Fernando del Pulgar. Both Spaniards are chroniclers of a world . . . in transition, contrasting an older warrior ethic with a newer concept of manhood associated with fame and virtuous life" *Dispositio* 16 (1991), 13–27.

[5] Joan Penzenstadler notes some of the similarities between Joyce's use of Ireland and Hinojosa's use of the Valley in "La

frontera, Aztlán, el barrio: Frontiers in Chicano Literature" in *The Frontier Experience and the American Dream.*

[6] See "Rolando Hinojosa-Smith" in *Contemporary Authors: Autobiography Series* for his account of the publishing history of his works and for a bibliography.

2

The Río Grande Valley
A Cultural Marriage

Hinojosa has said that his work is informed by an "idiosyncratic vision" ("Voice of One's Own" 13). This statement helps to explain the dualism inherent in his fiction, a characteristic occasioned by his own heritage, the two cultures of the Río Grande Valley, the tension between past and present, and the conflict within the Mexican-American community itself about self-identification and assimilation.[1] He says,

the very fact of my being the issue of my Texas Mexican father and his Anglo Texas wife, and because of my long life in Texas, I have seen and lived both cultures from a first-hand experience. . . . One language sup-planted the other for a while, but eventually they balanced each other out. What devel-oped from this, among other matters, was an idiosyncratic vision of the world; an aware-ness of differences and similarities. ("Voice of One's Own" 13)

It is true that Hinojosa grew up "within two cultures" ("Voice of One's Own" 12). But it is the Anglo culture in which he primarily lives and works, while more and more the old Mexican culture of his early years is becoming a memory, largely because—like all ru-ral American cultures—that culture, in its pure form, is dying out. As a high-tech, fast-paced world impinges on rural folk cultures, no matter what the ethnic make-up, those older cultures which only fifty or sixty years ago seemed stable begin to fragment. Hinojosa reveals through the *Klail City Death Trip Series* how necessary it has become for the Mexican American to face Anglo-American culture head on. He recognizes that the Mexican American is *American*. As a young-ster in a neighborhood school, he remembers singing the Mexican national anthem twice a day. However, he says, "We knew we were Mexican, but from this side of the river. . . . *Our reality was here*, and this was constantly brought home to us by World War II and by worries for my two older brothers who served in the naval and military services of this country" (*"La Prensa"* 127, italics mine). Héctor Torres writes of *The Valley* that we confront in it "a cultural heritage which is at once, Mexican *and* Anglo" ("Discourse and Plot" 84).[2] Hinojosa says that to depict the dual culture of the Valley honestly, he had to strive to avoid "romanticizing or sentimentalizing" the Mexican people ("Voice of One's Own" 14). His attempt to balance the two cultures produces in his novels a more balanced, richer vision than that of writers who depend heavily on cultural and ethnic stereotypes.

Despite Hinojosa's attempt to present both sides of Anglo-Hispanic life in his novels, many Chicano critics have analyzed his work from the limited viewpoint of the politicized Chicano movement. Chicano critics of the *Klail City Death Trip Series* most often either point out his reliance on Hispanic or Mexican forms or focus on the parts of his novels that describe Anglo exploitation of the Mexican.[3] José David Saldívar, likening Hinojosa to García Marquéz, says that the Chicano writer and critic has

> an image . . . of the writer that many Anglo-centric writers and intellectuals have lost— the writer who combines the traditional intellectual's commitment to language and image with the organic intellectual's commit-

ment to politics and revolution. (*Dialectics*
xiii)

Hinojosa himself has noted that the Chicano critic as
a rule is likely to work from a restricted viewpoint
and to impose restrictions on the Chicano writer. But,
he says of his work, "It isn't didactic. . . . Literature
should not find itself between walls" (Bruce-Novoa,
"Rolando" 56). Hinojosa's attempt to present a non-
didactic, balanced picture of Valley life has caused
some critics to see his work as "not political enough"
(Bruce-Novoa, "Rolando" 56). Hinojosa says, "If we
have scoundrels on the Anglo side, I'm going to bring
them out. By the same token, what scoundrels there
are on the Mexicano side should also be brought out"
(José David Saldívar, "Our Southwest" 184).

Hinojosa knows that "all serious literature"
makes an "assessment," or "evaluation," of society,
but he argues that asking a writer to produce work
that is "socially and politically relevant" does not allow him "much of a chance to be creative." He goes on
to say that criticism fails when it is "totalitarian"
(Bruce-Novoa, "Rolando" 59), and I think he would
disagree with Marciénne Rocard's argument that
Chicano literature must be highly political:

Chicano writing is no longer centered exclusively on the self because it would mean for-

getting the minority's history and struggle
for survival; it involves the reader and becomes a political act as it confronts him with
his cultural dilemma and awakens him to
national consciousness. Like all ethnic litera-
tures, Chicano literature is marked by ten-
sions, that is by a dialectical process of contradictions and opposing elements. Chicano
poetry, prose fiction, and drama are
dynamized by a number of polarities mirroring two antithetical views of life. The basic—
spatial and spiritual—opposition between
the *barrio*, the guardian of traditional values, and the dominant Anglo society modu-
lates into a series of oppositions: the opposition between yesterday (the Mexican past)
and today (the Anglo reality), between today
(a grim present) and tomorrow (a hopefully
better future). (34)

Ironically, Hinojosa's "better future," at least in an
individual, material sense, both for himself and his
characters, lies within the boundaries of the Anglo
community. Rocard's comments about the reader's
"cultural dilemma" assumes that a Chicano reader is
the only fit reader of Chicano literature. But Hinojosa
argues against such an ethnically restricted position
by saying of African-American writers,

When a Black says he suffers, I see and understand. When a Black critic tells me I don't
feel, then I must tell that critic, Black or not,
that if I don't *feel* then that is the writer's
fault. Pure and simple. (Bruce-Novoa, "Rolando" 51)

Hinojosa understands that literature—to be literature—must do more than merely present a political
or ethnic treatise. Rocard fails to comprehend what
is meant by Hinojosa's injunction that literature
should not build walls, and such comments as Héctor
Torres's that "Hinojosa's story-telling method itself
enables Chicano readers *in particular* [italics mine]
to see their Chicano heritage through the novel's plot-
structure" ("Discourse" 84–85) suggests that only a
Chicano reader can *truly feel* or understand the significance of Hinojosa's art. Again, these kinds of statements foster separatism at the author's expense.

Rocard speaks of "two antithetical views of life,"
while Hinojosa speaks of a vision that identifies both
similarities and differences. As to whether his work
tries to resolve the question of "the Texas-Anglos and
Texas-Mexicanos," Hinojosa answers that he is not
sure that there is an answer or resolution to the gap
between the two cultures: "It is a dialectic. It has to
continue" ("Sense of Place" 18). Yet the *Klail City*

Death Trip Series shows individual characters, if not whole communities, at least bridging that gap, if not filling it in, most notably through education and the passage of time.

Anglo critics, it is argued, with their limited knowledge of Mexican forms and oral tradition, may be tempted to focus only on similarities between Hinojosa's work and that of "mainstream" writers. And, as Joseph Sommers has argued, separating Chicano writers from their cultural backgrounds is just as limiting as is the political stance of many Chicano critics (32, 34). One must try, like Hinojosa himself, to attain a balance. Denying the importance of his characters' ethnicity would diminish Hinojosa's work, as does the assertion that the entire absolute value of the series rests on the fact of racial discrimination and little else.

Despite the fact that Hinojosa accepts the label "Chicano writer," it is difficult to fit him neatly into that politicized category. As Serge Ricard has said, "A vrai dire, il est temps de dissiper un malentendu: Rolando Hinojosa n'est pas un écrivan 'Chicano'—selon les norms definies" [To be honest, it is time to dispel a misunderstanding: Rolando Hinojosa is not a "chicano" writer, according to the defined standards"] ("Drogue" 169). The focal point of his work is neither political consciousness and pride in a mestizo heritage, nor is it an unblinking acceptance of the American dream. Despite the fact that his main characters achieve the American Dream, he valiantly attempts to keep them connected in some way to the old community. Yet a close analysis of the entire series reveals the steady progression of his major characters from the old culture toward the new. At the center of Hinojosa's work is a sense of wonder at the ways in which human beings of all races and cultures cope with the change that life insists on. In answer to the question "What are the outstanding qualities of Chicano literature?" Hinojosa says, "The presence of the Chicano and his endurance," that is, his ability to withstand the changing pressures of existence (Bruce-Novoa, "Rolando" 61). This is hardly the answer expected of a Chicano idealogue.

For Hinojosa and other "assimilated" Mexican Americans, one problem with the Chicano movement in its early stages was its emphasis on an Indian heritage, the focus on the downtrodden *campesino*, and the movement's hesitancy about assimilation into Anglo-American society. But, as Hinojosa has noted, "Since Nuevo Santander was never under the presidio system and since its citizens did not build missions that trapped and stultified the indigenous people, the latter remained there and, in time, settled down or were absorbed by the colonial population" ("Texas-Mexico Border" 98). So for Hinojosa, his culture, the Border culture, was a blended culture and had been for so long that any separation of the "Hispanic past" and the "Indian past" seemed impossible. As a result, Hinojosa has been unable to enter fully into the rhetoric of *Chicanismo*.

The Chicano movement, however, has sought to transcend the significant differences in attitude among Mexican Americans about such questions. In fact, the term "Chicano" has almost become an umbrella for diversity within the overall community. Sociologist Alice Reich claims a major unifying factor among Chicanos is that anyone who calls himself a Chicano is considered to be one, but the fact is that among people who use the word as "a term of self-identification," it may signify a variety of things (58). Given Hinojosa's Anglo heritage, these issues surely complicate his efforts to identify or place himself within the Mexican-American community.

In 1969, Professor Eliu Carranza criticized those "assimilated" or acculturated Mexican Americans who in any way "aided and abetted the preservation of the status quo," issuing a warning to such individuals:

> For those who identify strongly with the establishment, this revolution in thought and action may prove traumatic, for it is the establishment as it is now structured and those who would preserve that power structure

who have failed to understand the meaning
and the scope of the Chicano movement. (1)

Radical rhetoric such as Carranza's may have provided the impetus for Mexican-American academics
and writers such as Hinojosa to enter into the movement, at least on its academic fringes. Ironically,
Carranza is part of the academic establishment (now
an altered, but certainly not restructured establishment), and many of the most respected Chicano writers today are also academics. Most of them seem to
view success within the United States' university system as representing the highest—and most prag-
matic—goal of the Mexican American.[4] As Alfredo G.
de los Santos argues, "Mexican-American students
need to be encouraged to stay in school" (115), and he
goes on to lament the fact that so many Mexican-
American young people do not graduate from high
school and that among those who do, many attend
only community colleges which do not prepare them
for university-level work or the professions. He argues further that Mexican Americans must "continue
to insist that the educational system provide access
to social and economic mobility" (118).

This is a plea for inclusion, not in any way sepa-
ratist, similar to the pleas of those advocates of the
poorest, most isolated children of Appalachia. As
Mario T. García says of the Chicano movement of the

sixties and seventies, "From some perspectives, the strategy was radical and militant, but not un-American." He points out that the strategy worked: "It opened doors to college and universities. . . . The professional ranks of Mexican-Americans increased like never before" (*Dallas Morning News*, 19 Sept. 1993, A1, A20, A21).

It is most likely the liberalizing effect of a university education that kept Hinojosa and others away from the most radical aspects of the Chicano movement. Hinojosa's distance from the Chicano cry for separateness can be seen in his answer to the rather naive question, "Has formal education helped or hindered you as a writer?" Hinojosa answers,

> Formal education, in my case, has been an advantage: I tend to be wary of excesses in language or direction. Literature has so many good examples to draw from and so many bad ones to avoid. . . . Didacticism, totalitarian themes, boxed-in theses, and set propositions are intolerable and inexcusable for the serious writer of fiction and nonfiction, or of criticism for that matter. (Bruce-Novoa, "Rolando" 53)

In this single statement, Hinojosa sums up his attitude not only about literature, but also about the

demands of certain foundational elements of the
Chicano Movement that everything connected to the
Anglo establishment, including a traditional liberal
education, is suspect.

Though he is known as a "Chicano writer,"
Hinojosa clearly sees himself as a writer representing the peculiarly Spanish, Nuevo Santander heritage of his segment of the Río Grande Valley culture.
But Chicano critic and activist Felipe de Ortego y
Gasca, who claims the distinction of having fathered
the Chicano Renaissance, argues that the Chicano
movement

> came into being not in relation to the quaint
> and traditional Hispanic past of the Mexi-
> can American Southwest, but in the wake of
> growing awareness by Mexican Americans of
> their Mestizo past and their socio-political
> status. (5)

If Felipe de Ortega y Gasca is right, then Hinojosa's
point of view is in a sense only marginally Chicano.
The *Death Trip* does treat the socio-political status of
the Mexican American, but as part of a larger construct rather than as a plea for equity. With few ex-
ceptions, no matter what happens in the novels, no
matter how badly the Mexican American is abused
by the Anglo, Hinojosa's main characters can be seen

neither as victims nor as downtrodden individuals
unable to help themselves. Perhaps it is what
Hinojosa calls his strong sense of himself as a
"Borderer" which is responsible for this attitude
("Texas-Mexico Border" 95). As Héctor Calderón has
noted of *Generaciones y Semblanzas*, it "would never
develop a search for a Mexican or Chicano identity.
Because of historical circumstances . . . these characters already knew who they were" (14). He argues
that that is why *Generaciones* is "unlike other narratives of the Chicano Movement" (14), and yet
Hinojosa's characters are on a quest for a new identity.

Certainly Hinojosa's "vision" is quite distinct from
that of many other Chicano writers, including Rudolfo
Anaya.[5] Anaya, author of *Bless Me, Ultima*, which
has become one of the signature texts of Chicano phi-
losophy, says that as a Chicano artist he had to abandon the Anglo world of myth, compelling though it
might be. Instead, he says, he allowed his racial consciousness to take over:

> I dove into the common memory, into the dark
> and hidden past which was a lake full of trea-
> sure. The symbols I discovered had little to
> do with the symbols I knew from King
> Arthur's Court—they were new symbols,
> symbols I did not fully understand, but sym-

bols which I was sure spoke of the indigenous
American experience. The symbols and patterns I found connected me to the past, and
that past was not only my Hispanic, Catholic heritage; that past was also Indian Mexico.
I did what I had never been taught to do at
the university. I got in touch with myself, I
explored myself, and found I was a reflection
of that totality of life which had worked for
eons to produce me. (115)

In fact, it is the past of "Indian Mexico" that signifies
the epiphany that Anaya describes, not the European
past of which he was already conscious.

    Nowhere in Hinojosa does one find this kind of
open, explicit acknowledgement of such a connection
to the Indian past. Hinojosa's ethos seems peripheral
to the "center" that Anaya describes as the impetus
for his art, just as it ultimately bears little connection to the declaration that came out of the Chicano
Youth Liberation Conference of the late sixties, which
concluded that the Chicano was originally "a second
class citizen who was exploited by the Spanish Con-
quistador" and that the contemporary movement has
several related aims:

    Today the use of the term Chicano seeks to
    bring new dignity to Mexican Indian roots,

to uplift and liberate the concept of the working *peón* and *campesino*, and to introduce justice into the economic exploitation and racist attitude of the majority culture for the Mexican-American. (Montenegro 15)

Hinojosa has chosen to go beyond the stated goal of the Chicano Youth Liberation Conference effort. Though he does not fail to chronicle the hardships of the migrant laborers, and though economic and racial exploitation are a major part of the *Death Trip Series*, Hinojosa ultimately focuses on the segment of Mexican-American culture that he knows best: the upwardly mobile, at least partly assimilated group. As Donald Randolph has observed, "Neither Hinojosa nor those characters who are presented positively in his prose seem *trapped* in . . . agonies of cultural insecurity" [italics mine] ("Death's" 40).

Another problem in making sense of the many connotations attached to the term "Chicano" is that academics like Américo Paredes and Hinojosa apparently place the heart, if not the genesis, of the movement not with the inhabitants of the *barrio* or the migrant farm laborer, but with the upward mobility of men and women like themselves—people who have participated in the "American Dream," rather than those who have not become assimilated at all (Reich 508). Américo Paredes, speaking of the late Tomás

Rivera, another academic leader, says that Rivera
believed in a "community of leaders, of élites—a community of *mejicano* intellectuals serving as rallying
points and leaders for the rest of us" ("Nearby Places"
131). Rivera argues elsewhere that "In academia, the
anxiety to have a community, the urge to feel, sense,
and be part of a whole was the most constant preoccupation and need for Mexican-American students
and faculty alike" ("Mexican-American" 231). The
claim has been made that as early as the seventies
many Mexican Americans would refer to themselves
as Chicano only if they had been exposed to Anglo
culture in the university, where differences between
the two groups became more evident to them (Reich
67–68). Yet the trend is toward practical assimilation, even if a philosophical separatism persists.

Hinojosa refers to the Chicano Movement's literary aspect, saying that although it "passed itself off
as a people's literature," it is "actually a child of us,
the academicians who make up one of the last privi-
leged classes in our land" ("Chicano Literature" 41).
Again, Hinojosa's comment seems peripheral to the
inspiring rhetoric of other Chicanos, including the
claim of *El Plan Espiritual de Aztlán* that "we are a
bronze people with a bronze culture" (Montenegro 18).
Arnulfo D. Trejo, in *The Chicanos: As We See Ourselves*, attempts to define the term "Chicano":

> *Chicano* is the only term that . . . symboli-
> cally captures the historical past and signals
> a brighter future for the people of Aztlan.
> Aztlan was the homeland of the Aztecs. Its
> exact location has not yet been verified; none-
> theless, ancient traditions have placed it
> somewhere in the area encompassed by
> northwestern Mexico and the southwestern
> United States. Wherever it may be, Aztlan
> became a promised land and provided the
> spiritual unity needed by people in the
> Chicano movement. (xvii)

This type of rhetoric increases the difficulty of deter-
mining the philosophical stance of a writer like
Hinojosa, who says in an interview published in 1987
that the "American citizens" he is actually writing
about live in their "native land" and have "been here
since 1749" (Ricard, "An Interview" 195).

Hinojosa's comment about his Hispanic heritage—and the fact that not until the 1970s did any
real pride in the mestizo past begin to surface within
the Mexican-American community—brings up the
difficult subject of racial shame. Just as Anglo Americans before about 1970 often hid the fact of their
Native American blood, and just as many today would
deny having African-American blood, the Mexican
American traditionally downplayed his Indian blood

and identified himself as essentially European, Hispanic. As one historian has expressed it, after the
Spanish Conquest of the sixteenth century, Spanish
"ethnocentrism and excessive Christian zeal reduced
all things Indian to a level of shame" (Meyer and
Sherman 3). At least a remnant of this attitude lin-
gered well into the twentieth century. (This attitude
was similar as well to the Australian's shame over
his "convict" past.) Marilyn Montenegro asserts that
until recent years Mexican Americans as well as
Anglos used the term "Spanish" for Mexican Americans who were successful within Anglo society and
"Mexican" for those who were not. As people made a
"move from the *barrio*, to the Anglo community," some
passed as "Old Spanish," thereby making their way
into the higher realms of American society, a goal they
could achieve only if they did not look "Indian" (16).

      This "Spanish phenomenon" may be explained
by the fact that the Mexican American (like all minorities, ethnic or otherwise) feels the pressure to
conform to the dominant Anglo culture and simultaneously the pressure of negative stereotypes of the
"Mexican." As a result, he tries to distance himself
from the Mexican culture and the term "Mexican,"
which has come to signify a culture seen to be alien
to the dominant "American" culture. Hinojosa's characters more specifically appear to feel that there is a

real value in succeeding within the cultural framework of Anglo society.

This crisis of a dual identity has long existed in the Mexican-American community of the Río Grande Valley, just as it did in California and other places where there was a significant Hispanic population. Commenting on the racial makeup of the Valley, Hinojosa has clarified his personal position, even if he has avoided the issue as it has affected the inner workings of the Mexican-American community. He says that old-time Valley Mexicans, including his family, saw not only the Anglo but also the Mexican from the interior as "foreigners" ("This Writer's," 121). Hinojosa, whose father's family was among the original Spanish colonists, says that the border culture of the Valley is different from other Mexican-American cultures:

> For me and mine, history began in 1749 when the first [Spanish] colonists began moving onto the southern and northern banks of the Río Grande. That river was not yet a jurisdictional barrier and was not to be until almost one hundred years later; but, by then, the Border had its own history, its own culture, and its own sense of place. ("This Writer's" 121–22)

Granted, this border culture was a blended culture, encompassing the Indian and the Spanish, among whom intermarriage had been common. But it also became a blended culture by the intermarriage of Anglo and Mexican and by the proximity of two quite dissimilar cultures in a distinct geographical region. As Donald Chipman has noted, "the population of Texas at the close of the eighteenth century reflected ethnic mobility." He cites Alicia Tjorks's argument that there was "marked racial diversification, combined with and induced by an active biological and cultural miscegenation" (207).

George Banta, publisher of a small history of the Río Grande Valley written by Frank C. Pierce, writes of Anglos and *tejanos*, saying in the Preface that "at different periods in the past the country has been stirred by the dramatic episodes and the conflicts growing out of the meeting of two entirely dissimilar peoples in that land of cactus and mesquite" (*Texas' Last Frontier* n.p.). One might argue that the clash between the Spanish Conquistadors and the forces of Moctezuma was a more momentous meeting of "entirely dissimilar peoples" and that the internal conflict resulting from that earlier meeting has been just as dramatic as the conflict of the Anglo and *tejano*. As Donald Chipman has observed, the Indian had to learn "accomodation" upon the arrival of the Spaniard or suffer "elimination" (206). On a smaller scale,

the Texas Mexican of the Valley had to assimilate—
despite the difficulty of doing so—upon the arrival of
Anglo settlers, or in essence be crushed. Like the Indian before him, the Texas Mexican had the misfor-
tune of being caught in a culture whose very nature
made it vulnerable to the progressive dynamism of
the invading culture. The Mexican American, whether
of primarily Indian or Spanish descent, has main-
tained an awareness of at least these two identities—
a blended identity—so that beneath the broader
struggle of Mexican versus Anglo, there has been
another, perhaps less vocalized, internal racial
struggle. Historian Arnoldo de Léon, in writing of a
similar conflict in Mexico, reveals the strength of this
racial dichotomy. By the mid-nineteenth century, he
says, Mexicans were "searching for national regen-
eration":

> Liberals placed the blame for the country's
> ills on the bane of the colonial past and
> worked for a break with that legacy. Conser-
> vatives argued that the true national char-
> acter was to be found within a traditional
> Spanish heritage. Although their views dif-
> fered, both rejected Mexico's *mestizo* culture.
> ("Cultural Identity" 25)

A similar struggle emerged among the Mexican-American inhabitants of *la frontera*. This internal struggle, which may have reached its height during the last two or three decades, is never directly dealt with in Hinojosa's work. Still, whatever his personal outlook may be on the subject, it is an important one within the community that he writes about, and the natural defensiveness and contempt that the Mexican-American people feel for their oppressors is certainly evident in Hinojosa's work, and may in part be explained by the fact that the *tejanos* know it is their Indian past that the Anglo disdains.

A further consideration of how the twentieth-century Mexican-American writer responds to the dominant culture and his own past must take into account the question of language. Américo Paredes said in 1983 that if Spanish disappears from Chicano literature, the middle-sized tradition encompassing the *barrio* and the rural Little Traditions will become only a stage 'in a process of assimilation' ("Nearby Places" 132). Other Chicano critics, recognizing the multiple diversities within the Mexican-American community, argue that the Spanish language is the essential unifier for Chicanos and their literature.

In trying to determine what to write, and how to write, Hinojosa says that after much soul-searching, he decided "[I would] write what I had, in Spanish, and I decided to set it on the border, in the Valley"

("Sense of Place" 23). In making this decision, Hinojosa was simply following the old adage, "Write what you know." But the decision to write in Spanish was a much harder decision to make than it may seem, ensuring as it did that his audience in the United States would be quite limited. He says that writing in Spanish about experiences that would have been lived in Spanish lends a sense of truth that a text written in English would lack.

Nevertheless, though Hinojosa has continued to set his novels in the Valley, he soon abandoned Spanish for English. The decision to do so was complicated by the desire to maintain a sense of truth and the linguistic fidelity so important to the self-identification of ethnic cultures, and the realization that to become a recognized writer in his native country, the United States, he must produce work in English. He has said, "I see myself as a writer, and . . . I try to get published" (Bruce-Novoa, "Rolando" 55). The reason he gives for shifting to English is that he started to write about experiences that would have been lived in English; in a 1987 interview, he said, however,

> yo no vivo in exilo, yo vivo en mi país. Yo prefiero escriber en español si el ambiente que estoy describiendo es de habla hispana, pero, así que entra el mundo norteamericano, el inglés es la lengua más natural. Fíjese,

cuando nos reunimos tres o cuatro colegus
mexico-Americanos en un despagos char-
lamos en español, nos reimos, gastamas
bromas . . . de repente se empieza a hablar
de temos profesionales y automáticamente
pasamos a hablar todas en inglés. El idioma
profesional, el de los negocios, el de las
docencia, el es inglés. [I do not live in exile, I
live in my country. I prefer to write in Spanish if the environment I'm describing is a
Spanish-speaking one, but, when one enters
the world of the North American, English is
the more natural language. Actually, when
three or four Mexican-American colleagues
meet in an office, we chat in Spanish, laughing, making jokes . . . suddenly one begins to
speak of professional things, and automati-
cally we cross over to speak entirely in English. The professional, business, and
educational language is English.] (Riera 14)

There is, however, evidence that this is not the only
reason for the change. As Hinojosa said in 1974,
American publishers are not likely to publish a novel
written in Spanish, so "the Chicano writer has been
forced to write in English" ("Mexican-American" 424).
Hinojosa clearly understands the practical problems
associated with writing in Spanish. He also under-

stood that there was some stigma attached to writing in English during the early days of the Chicano movement, a stigma that may not have entirely vanished. In 1986, Marciénne Rocard said that "a Chicano who speaks English is trapped in the language of the oppressor and 'dissolves into the melting-pot'" (35); in 1987, José Limón, in arguing for binguilism for the Mexican American said, "in the face of barbarism, we must learn English" (25).

Besides concern for his audience, Hinojosa's decision to shift to English allowed him to recapture exactly the tone of his original work. Recreating his own works in English enabled him to maintain control of his "voice." Despite his concerns about the lack of Spanish in Chicano literature, Américo Paredes has praised Hinojosa for rewriting his work in English and has suggested that it was a kind of "romantic nationalism" that first impelled Hinojosa and other Mexican-American writers to work in Spanish ("Nearby Places" 134). Bruce-Novoa argues that language should not be a "test" of a Chicano writer's fidelity:

> We should not ask if Chicano writers are loyal or not to Spanish, but rather, what is the language of preference. Chicano writers, like any writers, tend to use the language they control best. If that happens to be English, as in

the majority of cases, then that is the writer's
native language. After all, Chicano writers
are either citizens or permanent residents of
this country and have a perfect right to claim
its native heritage. ("Cultural" 26)

Bruce-Novoa thinks that "writing itself" is most significant to a creative writer—but perhaps not to "poli-
ticians or polemicists" ("Cultural" 26). Because
Hinojosa is *not* a politician or polemicist, he has been
able to choose for himself, as an artist, the language
in which he wishes to express his art.

In a 1988 interview, Hinojosa clarified his position on the language issue by saying that "it's a narrow view on the part of some activitists" to assume
that if a Chicano writer uses English, then he cannot
create a valid picture of Chicano life (Dasenbrock 4).
He also opens up his potential readership by saying,

You have to trust the reader, always. I speak
German, but not well, and I read German,
but not well, but I've read everything by
Heinrich Böll, and I think Leila Vennewitz,
the translator, transmits to me exactly what
Heinrich Böll wants transmitted. If I were
to take the extremist attitude, then I would
never read him or Günter Grass, or anybody
else. (Dasenbrock 4)

Though the issue of language is a sensitive one for many Mexican Americans, the historical reality for Hispanics in this country is that to break free of the negative aspects of the *barrio*, they must break through the language barrier. As Hinojosa says, "This is not a Spanish-speaking country for the most part" (Bruce-Novoa, "Rolando" 57). Hinojosa shows his major characters breaking through this barrier, which suggests that he sees this falling away from the *mejicano* culture as a good thing for the individual, if not for the community. But most likely he sees it as inevitable, given the history of our time, demonstrating again his grasp of history's implications for the individual human being.

In any case, Hinojosa and other assimilated, outspoken Mexican Americans, particularly academics, are in a unique position, one which often muddies the issue of whether they are latecomers who have tried to appropriate the vigor of the Chicano movement after the fact, or whether they have in fact been the heartbeat of the movement. Answers are not immediately evident, but the fact remains that many assimilated Mexican American writers and academics, whether they can rightfully claim to have given birth to the Chicano movement, have certainly fostered its literature. Whether they borrowed or created the energy of the movement may be a moot question, but it is always enlightening to a student

of Chicano literature to assess how any particular
Mexican-American writer fits into such a politically
charged category.

---

[1] Hinojosa also explains his dual heritage by saying, "Pero
mi caso es aún máas complicado porque soy Hinojosa, pero mi
segundo apellido es Smith. Pertenzio a otra minoria dentro de la
minoría, los que tenemos un apellido español y otro ingles." ["But
my case is even more complicated because I am Hinojosa, but my
second name is Smith. I belong to another minority within the
minority, those of us who have one Spanish name and another
English."] Miguel Riera, "El Otro Sur: Entrevista con Rolando
Hinojosa."

[2] *Newsweek* writers Jerry Adler and Tim Padgett claim that
the "Mexican American border . . . has undergone what University of Arizona historian Oscar Martinez calls 'a profound, silent
integration' of its two halves." "Selena Country," *Newsweek*.

[3] Most of the essays in the *Rolando Hinojosa Reader* fall into
this category. See also Alurista's "Cultural Nationalism and
Chicano Literature" in *Missions in Conflict: Essays on U.S.-Mexi-
can Relations and Chicano Culture*. See also Ramón Saldívar, "A
Dialectic of Difference."

[4] See Alfredo G. de los Santos, "Facing the Facts about Mexican America"; Tomás Rivera, "Statement of Personal Outlook on
the Future of American Higher Education"; and Rolando Hinojosa,
"Tomás Rivera (1935–1984)."

[5] Serge Ricard says "au contraire de Rudolfo Anaya . . . la
quête d'une identité ou l'exploration d'un passé mythique ne sont
nullement des préoccupations centrales." ["Unlike Rudolfo Anaya,

the quest for an identity or the explorations of vanished myth are by no means Hinojosa's main concerns."] Ricard uses the term "identity" to refer to that sort of identity that Anaya speaks of in *A Yankee*, not the sort of newly created identity that demands a surrender of ethnicity. ("Un Art de la Survie: Chicanismo et religion dans l'oeuvre de Rolando Hinojosa.")

3

Marking the Path
The *Death Trip* in Sequence

Rolando Hinojosa did not begin writing fiction with the conscious intention of producing a sequence novel, but by the time he wrote *Korean Love Songs*, "the idea of a *Klail City Death Trip* was absolutely fixed" (José David Saldívar, "Our Southwest" 181). Hinojosa has noted how the *Death Trip Series* evolved: In 1972, a brief sketch called "Por esas cosas que pasan" ("for those things which are past/gone") was published, after which he wrote "Una vida de Rafa Buenrostro" ("A life of Rafe Buenrostro"), "Vidas y milagros" ("Lives and miracles"), and "Estampas" ("Images/Sketches"). These four short pieces became *Estampas del valle y otras obras*

(Sketches of the Valley and Other Works). He produced
three more short works, "Notas de Klail City y sus
Alrededores, II," ("Notes on Klail City and its Envi-
rons"), "Brechas Viejas y Nuevas" ("Trails Old and
New"), and "Generaciones y semblanzas" ("Generations and portraits/sketches"), which ultimately—in
1987—became the novel *Klail City*. Writing these
short pieces made Hinojosa realize the significance
of history to his art, particularly the history of the
Mexican American in the Texas Valley.

That this particular chronology should mark the
beginnings of the *Death Trip* sequence in Hinojosa's
own mind is not surprising. He deals primarily with
the concepts of continuity and change, and their importance from both the historical and personal perspectives. In the early works, the old ways of the past
play a predominant role. Hinojosa depicts them as
the shaping forces of the personalities and characters of both individuals and the Mexicano community at large. Yet, as Robert Morris, one of the first
critics to treat the sequence novel as a literary genre,
suggests, even in a sequence where there is a particular and possibly overriding focus on history, "the
historical background is generally dominated by the
fictional foreground" (xv).

Hinojosa teeters between the two, but rarely gives
way anywhere in his work to strict, explicit reliance
on historical fact. For example, except for the facts

about the Mexican Revolution, the dominance of the "rinches" (Texas Rangers) in the Valley during the late nineteenth and early twentieth centuries, and the Korean War, the rest of the *Klail City Death Trip Series* is anecdotal, fictionalized, though no doubt much of what Hinojosa describes is a recounting of "facts," of actual events which he either witnessed firsthand or which were part of an oral tradition during his formative years. Still, *Estampas*, the works that became *Klail City*, and parts of *Claros Varones*, perhaps more than any others, establish the motif of the "glorious past" and a coherent community, and present a picture of continuity that stands in bold relief against the world of change found in the later works. It is true that history is significant to most writers of the sequence novel, including Hinojosa, who, in speaking of his writing career, says, "It was a matter of luck in some ways . . . but mostly it was the proper historical moment; it came along, and I took it" ("Sense of Place" 23–24). Hinojosa is speaking specifically of the early 1970s and the flowering of the Chicano movement, but he might just as well be speaking of the entire history of the Río Grande Valley, a history that he takes for his subject.

The phenomenon of the sequence novel is not new, having been exploited to good effect in the nineteenth century by novelists like Balzac, Proust, Trollope, and others. In the twentieth century, the form has been especially popular in Britain and America. Ford Madox Ford, C. S. Lewis, Doris Lessing, C. P. Snow, Anthony Powell, and John Updike have all extended the limits of the sequence novel. In addition to the form's popularity with serious novelists, it has become one of the staples of such genre-fiction writers as Conan Doyle, Agatha Christie, Dorothy Sayers, Rex Stout, and Ross Macdonald, who reprise the same characters in novel after novel.[1]

In America, of course, the earliest practitioner of the sequence novel was probably James Fenimore Cooper, whose *Leatherstocking Tales* take the main character through five adventure narratives held together by Natty Bumpo's movement across an ever-disappearing frontier. Interestingly, Hinojosa's novel sequence deals with themes similar to Cooper's. Other American writers who have worked in the sequence genre include Faulkner with his Yoknapatawpha novels and John Updike with the "Rabbit" series. Even William Saroyan, in the collection of vignettes that make up *My Name is Aram*, creates a work with several characteristics of the sequence.

One common element among novelists such as Balzac, Cooper, and Updike is that they write about a rapidly changing world, and about individual characters who must confront historical—and consequently personal—change. Cooper depicts the transformation of the American wilderness that took

place during the life of his main character. He also
reveals the transformation of America from the
Jeffersonian to Hamiltonian ideal, from an agrarian
society to a merchant society. Faulkner works with
the devastating change from Old South to New South,
and, in many ways, is lamenting the same things that
Cooper decried a hundred years earlier. Updike creates a modern middle-class hero living in a world in
which change is both unrelenting and soul-searing.
Trollope, like Balzac, depicts the upheaval of the nineteenth century as he shows the change in English
society after the Industrial Revolution—the increas-
ingly blurred social and class hierarchy, particularly
between the wealthy industrialist and aristocratic
classes, the diminished power and influence of the
Church, and a nostalgia for a quiet way of life possible only in a few small corners of England. Ford
Madox Ford chronicles the dramatic change brought
about in British society by World War I. Doris Lessing,
in *Children of Violence*, depicts the struggle for independence in Rhodesia. Even P. G. Wodehouse's comic
series is an effort to capture a small world that existed for a very short time—Bertie Wooster's world
could not long withstand the pressures of the outside
world, a dynamic, sometimes terrifying world against
which even Jeeves could not prevail.

Such preoccupation with change characterizes
Hinojosa's exploration of the Texas Valley in the *Klail*

City Death Trip Series. As Hinojosa writes in *Klail City* and several other works, "Nothing lasts a hundred years" (143). In the Río Grande Valley, more change came about during the period from the 1940s to the 1990s than had happened during the hundred years before. What Robert Morris says about the mid-twentieth-century British sequence novel holds true for Hinojosa's *Death Trip Series*. He argues that it is concerned with

> the image and impact of society upon the individual; the quest after a vanishing ideal; the search for a personal *modus vivendi* within the social and political *modus vivendi*; the closing circle of freedom in an age constricted with varieties of determinism—an admittedly existential proposition; or, finally, the displacement of the glorious myths of humanity by the ogre of history. (xviii)

Even though the sequence novel was clearly established in the nineteenth century, it has become a major subgenre only in the twentieth because it is a literary form that is very much concerned not only with personal change, but also with historical change. The nineteenth century experienced great upheavals resulting from the political, social, and scientific revolutions of the eighteenth century, culminating in the Industrial Revolution. The twentieth century has had to confront even more unrelenting change, beginning with World War I and continuing to the present time. In this century, the broad sweep of history certainly provides the writer of a sequence novel a dramatic backdrop against which to place his characters. Unlike Eliot's Prufrock, a character in a sequence novel rarely has time for indecision as history presses upon him.

This pressure to act is felt by Hinojosa's Mexican-American characters; they are forced to confront Anglo-American society first by American expansionism and daily social contact, and later by World War II, changing attitudes, the Civil Rights movement, and mutual dependencies of all sorts. Hinojosa is deeply interested in this history: "I have [a penchant] for looking at society in general and making telling comments about it as time and the society change in Belken. . . . I don't think I could ever write a novel without referring to some form of history" (qtd. in José David Saldívar, "Our Southwest," 183–84). A necessary connection between history and character development is common in the sequence novel. Robert Morris sums up the task of the novelist who "flirts with etiology, riveting one eye on patterns of time, the other on patterns of timelessness, while focusing both on the causes and reasons for the individual's moral, aesthetic, psychological or social growth" (xiii–xiv).

The novelist must at once embrace and eschew history and historical time if he is to capture that peculiar phenomenon of human experience, the tension between continuity and change. He must *use* history to demonstrate the motif of continuance and change, but he must also *rise above* it if he is to produce "art" and not simply "transcribe history" (Robert Morris xv). This is precisely what Hinojosa attempts in the *Klail City Death Trip Series*. The historical past—which is sometimes used explicitly but which most often lurks on the parameters of events—is Hinojosa's way of "flirting with etiology," and his belief that the same things happen to different people at different times in history confirms his awareness of change and continuance ("Sense of Place" 24).

Another explanation for the "phenomenal" (Robert Morris xiv) proliferation of the sequence novel in twentieth-century fiction may simply be that the pressure of relentless change has created in the population at large a desire for characters who do not disappear after one novel or one segment of a television series. (The serial novel of the nineteenth century fulfilled the audience's desire for a continuing story, but some writers, like Dickens, did not continue their characters beyond the three-decker serial novel.)

The popularity of the "Rocky" movies, "Lethal Weapon III," and the many versions of the "Halloween" horror movies attests to our need for continuity, even in light entertainment. A sequence ensures continuing interest, and what happens to us when we become attached to a television series is the same thing that happens to us when we become engrossed in a sequence novel: ultimately, plot is less important than a character's response to what happens. The same is true of Hinojosa's fiction: "My stories are not held together by the *peripeteia* or the plot so much as by *what* the people who populate the stories say and how they say it, how they look at the world out and the world in" ("Sense of Place" 21). We reach a point at which we watch the television show to observe the characters; we are attached to them, we talk about them as if they were "real" people. (This is why the villains on soap operas are sometimes accosted on the streets.)

Though a fine distinction exists between who does what and what happens, once we feel a sense of familiarity toward the characters, we become far less critical of the plot than we were when we first began watching the series or reading the sequence. Once we have become attached to a character, we are willing to tolerate the slightest—sometimes even silliest—plot imaginable, because our interest is no longer deeply connected to what happens, but rather to how the character responds to what happens. Even though the sequence novel *may* develop character in a strictly traditional sense, it may also, like Hinojosa's, broaden the perspective to depict a journey which follows more or less the Jungian pattern:

> The myth of psychic reintegration: the escape, the plunge, the journey, the dangerous and saving encounters, the magical guidance to the journey's end, and the final healing of the personality. (Lewis 39)

Structurally, the *Death Trip Series* generally follows this order, and though it may leave us wondering whether the personalities involved can ever be truly healed, it does depict a similar quest. At the same time it details another aspect of the Jungian pattern: "the necessary transforming shocks and sufferings, the experiments and errors—in short, the experience—through which maturity and identity may be arrived at" (Lewis 61).

The *Klail City Death Trip Series* illustrates all the phenomena of the sequence novel. Historically, it reveals how the twentieth century, particularly the post-World War II period, signaled a dynamic change in the life of the Texas Valley. Not only did the Mexican American find himself in the position to challenge old ways and old prejudices that had bound him economically and socially for well over a hundred years, but the Anglo also had to face up to a world in which those who had been denied basic opportunities were now demanding them, and, in many cases, getting them. At the same time, internal conflict, brought about by a variety of factors, characterized relationships among members of the Mexican-American community. One of the most significant of these is the Mexican American's efforts to retain his ethnic identity while assimilating himself into the Anglo culture during the post-war period, a time when individual Mexican Americans began to penetrate the dominant socio-economic system (Simmons 159, 492, 524). This was a process not always smiled upon even by the Mexican American. There were ways and then there were ways; Hinojosa shows the toadying Ira Escobar, who is an Anglo's handpicked candidate for county commissioner, as taking the wrong route. Ira loses the respect of those who matter in the Mexican-American community, and he ultimately loses his wife Becky, who in turn begins her career the wrong way, but finally gives up the women's club and goes into business with Viola Barragán. Characters like Rafe and Jehú at first seem to infiltrate the Anglo community while remaining attached to the *mejicano* world, but later they appear to become almost fully assimilated within it, at least on the surface.

To analyze these conflicts and changes within the Mexican-American community itself, Hinojosa has to get beyond the Anglo-Mexican conflict, but in order to present a true picture of the Valley he cannot fully ignore the racial conflict. He reveals his ability to *transcend* the race issue in *Klail City* when he describes the Purdys of Pinconning, Michigan, who created "a clean, well-lighted place" for the migrant workers from Texas (69); he also transcends the Mexican victim/Anglo victimizer mentality when he describes the Leguízamons, who hired Mexican nationals to kill Rafe Buenrostro's father, don Jesus.

Hinojosa clearly understands that all humans are corruptible. As Joan Penzenstadler says, "We know that Chicano culture and people have as many flaws as Anglo culture and people," but much of Chicano literature, stressing the "native American side of the ancestry" is dealing in Indian myth, which is "by nature ethnocentric" (160). One of Hinojosa's distinctions is that this particular myth is rarely manifest in his work. To remain faithful to history rather than produce mere propaganda, Hinojosa has to present a myriad of views not only on the race conflict, but also on the various other conflicts within the Mexican culture. This necessity for a changing point of view helps to explain Hinojosa's adoption of his distinctive style; yet what he says about his method—the lack of plot—

suggests that he is intuitively aware of the way in which a reader's interest works within a novel sequence. Here he simply reiterates the idea that, in the novel sequence, the study of a character's "perceptions and values and decisions" ("Sense of Place" 21) is what the reader is ultimately engaged in; hence the usefulness of recurring characters in changing circumstances.

Hinojosa is not alone in perceiving the *Death Trip Series* as a sequence. He has said, "There's no novelistic statute that says I have to end a novel in one tome or two" (Bruce-Novoa, "Rolando" 60) and asserts that "I'm writing a long piece of work in several volumes" (Ricard, "Interview" 194). José D. Saldívar argues that the *Death Trip Series* is "structurally . . . a multidimensional, historical novel" ("*Klail*" 49). Juan Bruce-Novoa says that

> through the brief episodes, the short stories, and even the poetry into which his works are structured, he is slowly and unconventionally creating a novel on a grand scale. The pieces are obviously interrelated, in the manner of a mosaic; eventually they will reveal the cast pattern of a tightly interlocked whole. ("Rolando" 50)

Robert Morris says that critics tend to view the sequence novel in one of two ways:

> For some critics the sequence novel is not really *a* novel at all, but a number of books loosely strung together. For others it is *a* novel, but at its most infirm, hobbling along, with history as a kind of telescoping truth that can be lengthened and shortened at whim should the author's fancy or imagination give out. (xvii)

One reviewer, whose attitude clearly reflects his prejudice, asks whether all Hinojosa's material "cannot be sustained long enough to complete one fat *novel* on the Valley" (DuBose 16).[2]

Ostensibly, everyone knows that "style, like content, is intimately involved with form," but "how one actually affects the other is a new and complex matter when related to the novel sequence" (Robert Morris xviii). Hinojosa's personal unwillingness to comment on the action of his novels reveals his intention of leaving the commentary to the voices that people his novels. Hinojosa is not in any way absent from his novels, for they are essentially autobiographical, but he strives to disguise his own voice by utilizing many voices. As Elizabeth Hardwick says of

Virginia Woolf's work, it is "all chorus and no plot"
(136). Often, Jehú's voice seems to speak for both himself and Rafe, the two major yet essentially enigmatic
characters who seem almost interchangeable in the
Klail City sequence. In *Korean Love Songs* and *The
Useless Servants*, Rafe seems to speak for both himself and Jehú. These two characters apparently answer Hinojosa's need to express the duality of his
vision, for they are clearly counterparts of a single,
perhaps archetypal, figure engaged in a single quest
to come to terms with the world around him, and they
provide an element of continuity within the sequence
as a whole. Equally important to thematic continuity
is the figure of P. Galindo. It is P. Galindo who is often responsible for bringing the past to life in the early
novels. It is P. Galindo who insists on remembering—
and causing others to remember—the past, a past
described for Rafe by Esteban Echevarría, who says
it is "dead and gone" (*Claros Varones* 206). Up through
Claros Varones, Echevarría, who dies at age eighty-
seven in the 1950s, is the "storyteller," in the sense of
historian or wise man, for the Mexican-American community; P. Galindo, who is somewhat younger, is the
"keeper of memories" who writes the oral histories
down. Significantly, P. Galindo also dies at the end of
Dear Rafe, in essence making way for the "new" men
(who are somewhat younger than Galindo), Rafe and

Jehú, who carry the past in their souls but who must now shoulder the burdens of the present as well.

One of the ways in which the writer of a sequence novel creates continuity is to use a group of characters, all of whom are more or less related in terms of their social status and background and/or family history. A fairly small—and manageable—cast of characters will appear in a particular novel, with some members of the larger group appearing in adjunct roles (perhaps only their names will be mentioned). In another novel, the roles will be exchanged, and exchanged again in yet another work, etc. James Fenimore Cooper, for example, takes a single hero through a series of novels in which he is surrounded by a core of characters that remains mostly static (though characters may die, marry, or disappear) but in which the hero is introduced to new characters and new situations in each novel. Anthony Powell's *Dance to the Music of Time* is another such work. Here Nicholas Jenkins, who is also the narrator, is clearly the focus of the entire sequence. From his days at school, and his first observations of Widmerpool through army life, marriage, his career as a writer, it is Nicholas Jenkins who provides the commentary—and the interest—for the world Powell is creating.

Hinojosa borrows something from both of these methods in his *Klail City Death Trip Series*. He clearly

sees Rafe Buenrostro and Jehú Malacara as his heroes, and they do provide the sometimes fragile thread
of continuity that the sequence exhibits, though they
are not really the center of the work in the way that
Nicholas Jenkins is the absolute center of Powell's
work. Nevertheless, much of what Robert Morris says
of Powell's *A Dance to the Music of Time* and Nicholas Jenkins is applicable to Hinojosa's *Death Trip*, and
Morris's description of Nicholas could be a description of Jehú Malacara:

> Even when "involved," Nick keeps his dis-
> tance and hangs in the background, more
> concerned with what is happening around
> him than to him. . . . [A] faithful narrator, he
> is no facetious historian. He accepts experi-
> ence with no thought of forecasting its long-
> range significance. Nick reacts with sympa-
> thy, amusement, or mild astonishment to the
> things happening around him, for he refuses
> to be daunted by change and is, in the last
> analysis, only fascinated by it. (124)

Unlike some characters who are caught in the past,
Nick Jenkins, like Jehú

> charts a course between extremes, measur-
> ing the smallest signs or gestures against

contemporary standards and holding fast to sensible and humane values. From his shadowy beginnings as a narrator and his often obvious role as author-surrogate, he has emerged into a full-blown hero; far above and beyond things, he has learned how a student of history and society should confront the uses of the past and men. (125)

This description fits the young Jehú of *The Valley*, as well as the more mature Jehú found in parts of *The Valley*, *Dear Rafe*, and the concluding pages of *Klail City*. When Jehú and Rafe attend their twentieth high school reunion, Jehú remembers the snobbery and racial conflict of their high school days, but he concludes with these words, "we all laugh about it now. And we should. And we do . . . no pain, no debt, nothing lasts a hundred years" (*KC* 142–43).[3]

Despite Hinojosa's use of recurring characters, in at least *The Valley*, *Klail City*, and *Claros Varones*, the intermittent focus on Rafe and Jehú alternates with the intrusion of the community, of a multilayered cacophony of recurring voices, which is representative of Hinojosa's multiple-exposure style. (Even in *Dear Rafe*, the community intrudes in the "reportage" section.) Hinojosa's method fragments history and character simultaneously, in much the same way Faulkner's work does, so that it is difficult for a reader

ever to stand on firm ground in relation to the "story"
being told or in relation to the character (frequently
unidentified and sometimes unidentifiable) who is
speaking.

Mark Busby has noted Faulkner's influence on
Hinojosa.[4] Borrowing Faulkner's phrase, Hinojosa
says that he is the "sole owner and proprietor" of
Belken County ("Faulknerian Elements" 16). If a similarity exists between Faulkner and Hinojosa, it is not
that Hinojosa's work is of the same dimension as
Faulkner's, but rather that they are both American
regionalists, and that their subject matter is similar.
Faulkner's fiction relies heavily on the presence of a
disintegrating "aristocracy," just as Hinojosa's suggests that a brief, glorious past existed for the Spanish *grandee* in the Texas Valley. Faulkner and Hinojosa both believe in the possibility of an aristocracy
in American culture because they both believe that
an aristocracy *did exist* in the past. This belief, accurate or inaccurate, sets them apart from most other
American regionalists. In addition, the idea of the old
Mexican community as a coherent entity parallels
Faulkner's vision of the Old South as a unit,
unfragmented by war and time and change.

The difference between them lies in their attitudes toward change. Faulkner clearly disparages the
direction the New South is taking. Hinojosa, though

he recognizes and laments the loss of the old culture, sees change in the Valley from a broader perspective. The term "cultural values" has become almost a cliché among critics of Chicano literature, and the loss of such values is routinely lamented. However, Robert Morris observes that the writer of a novel sequence may see "decay" as creative opportunity. He says that the "disintegration of values" is a "motif of the century," and explains that the novelist may view this decay differently from the professional historian or casual observer:

> To the historian, such decay may emerge as a single, simple fact, as, say, the fall of an empire is a fact. The totalities involved in accounting for it, however, are never as factual or as simple as one might like them to be. The historian may see decay as the most contributive factor of change. The novelist . . . knows that it is only one part of change; growth is another, individual growth that is rarely accounted for in the historic process and is often lost in the indifference and inexorability of time. (125)

The growth of the individual personality which change necessitates—along with the growth of the

Mexican-American community—is a major motif in
the *Death Trip*. The chrysalis is shed, and along with
it goes much that was comfortable and secure.

Despite the difference in outlook, both Faulkner
and Hinojosa seem to feel the need to *explain* their
worlds, not just describe them; their efforts to define
and even justify their cultures are not really surprising in light of the essentially "un-American" nature
of those cultures, as they are perceived by the population at large. Both peoples have been cast as slow-
moving, lethargic—the sharecropper of the South a
neat counterpart to the migrant worker. Faulkner and
Hinojosa go about their explanations in quite different ways, with quite different results, but, as Mark
Busby has said, they both realize the usefulness of
the sequence—and shifting perspectives—in their
effort to create an art that can explain these regional
cultures ("Faulknerian" 106).

Another American whose work even more closely
parallels Hinojosa's is the Armenian-American William Saroyan, best known for his short fiction. In
works such as *My Name is Aram*, Saroyan is struggling to do what both Faulkner and Hinojosa are doing—explaining an "atypical" culture to the dominant,
typical one. The Armenian community in California
was plagued by problems similar to those of the Mexican-American community in South Texas, such as the
language barrier. Both Hinojosa and Saroyan depict

a people who believe in their greatness and their past, but who find themselves second-class citizens, reduced to menial and agricultural labor.

In addition, Hinojosa's style mirrors Saroyan's. Saroyan's rather sentimental, nostalgic world-view, as opposed to Hinojosa's ironic, sometimes almost cynical point of view, cannot obscure the similarities between the two writers. Saroyan's stories seem randomly collected, exhibiting a "lack of continuity, form, or unity" (Spiller 1333). These very words might be used to describe Hinojosa's work as well, though both Saroyan and Hinojosa do provide sufficient historical continuity, that "relentless backdrop" that Robert Morris speaks of, and the comfort of a recurring character or characters to give a relatively coherent form to their fictions.

Both are concerned with an ethnic community caught in an identity crisis as the world changes. Hinojosa's Valley, as depicted in the early novels, is almost a mirror of Saroyan's Armenian community in Fresno, California, during roughly the same period. Both authors are concerned with the same problems: how does one group live an authentic life under the control of the dominant group? Or, to put it another way, how do the people who make up a little tradition live in the face of an often repressive "big" tradition? The Armenians faced the problems of a dual language and culture just as the Texas Mexicans of the period did. In fact, Saroyan's prefatory "Note" to *My Name Is Aram* (a series written in the 1930s but covering the period from 1915 to 1925) could almost, with a few changes, stand as the preface to Hinojosa's Klail City novels. Saroyan says that the stories cover a time before the author began "to inhabit the world as a specific person" and before he "had forsaken his native valley for some of the rest of the world. . . . " The same, of course, is true of Hinojosa's early work. He says, "I had left the Valley . . . only to return to it in my writing" ("Sense of Place" 24).

Saroyan continues,

> While no character in this book is a portrait of any real person living or dead, as the saying is, neither is any person in this book a creation of fiction. No member of my family will be able to find himself in any one person in the book, but at the same time none will be able to find himself wholly *absent* from any one of them. If this is true of us, it is probably true of everyone else, which in the opinion of the writer is proper. (Saroyan, vii)

These comments are particularly apt in describing the *Death Trip* as well as *My Name Is Aram*. Hinojosa, as he appears in the guise of his surrogate authors, is a composite character. He is not Rafe, Jehú, P.

Galindo, etc., but all of them in one way or another. But at the same time, the *Death Trip* has a universality that transcends the regional motif, so that if these characters *contain* Hinojosa, then they also contain all the rest of us or "everyone else," as Saroyan claims.

The use of the author as character is another similarity between Saroyan's sequence of stories about Fresno Armenians and Hinojosa's stories about *tejanos*. Saroyan says in his "Note": "As to whether or not the writer himself is Aram Garoghlanian, the writer cannot very well say. He will, however, say that he is not, certainly, *not* Aram Garoghlanian" (x). Hinojosa's characters Rafe and Jehú are both versions of the author himself; Hinojosa might also say that he is both, but certainly not *either* Rafe Buenrostro or Jehú Malacara. Saroyan's Aram and Hinojosa's Jehú/Rafe see the world in much the same way—with a vision that is a mixture of bewilderment and uncanny observation. These characters all have some of Huckleberry Finn in them, for they know more as children than children are supposed to; yet they know that mysteries abound in the adult world, and they only partially perceive that they live in a world under siege by the "big tradition."

Saroyan's style is also similar to Hinojosa's, especially the little aside "as the saying is" and his references to "the writer." Saroyan's Fresno and Hinojosa's Klail are so alike that it is impossible to believe that Hinojosa has not read Saroyan. In the "Note," Saroyan says of his little corner of the world:

> It was, as a matter of fact, and probably still is, as good a town as any in the world for a writer to be born into, being neither too large nor too small, too urban or too rural, too progressive or too backward . . . but in all these things, as well as in all others, and in several unknown anywhere else in the world, so delicately, so nicely, and so delightfully balanced as to give the spirit of the growing writer almost exactly the right proportion of severity and warmth, and firmness and flexibility. . . . Consequently, the writing of this book, more than the writing of any of the writer's other books, has been without effort, strain, or any other kinds of wretchedness said to be experienced by writers as eager, if not more eager than this writer to send a message down the ages, "as the saying is." (viii)

In the epigraph to *The Valley*, Hinojosa writes, "what follows, more likely as not, is a figment of someone's imagination; the reader is asked to keep this disclaimer in mind. For his part, the compiler stakes no claim of responsibility; he owns and holds the copyright but little else." Obviously, Hinojosa shares the same fey sense of humor.

If Saroyan's short stories seem at times like sketchily connected vignettes, then the "sections" of Hinojosa's novels appear just as loosely connected. In *My Name is Aram*, the stories do not really form a pattern, with Saroyan delineating Aram's growth as he moves from "a small boy" to his adolescence, when he longs for the body-building course offered by Mr. Strongfort and when he drives a car—Locomotive 38's Packard—for the first time. The presence of Aram's grandparents and the appearance of his Uncle Khosrove in both the first story, "The Summer of the Beautiful White Horse," and the next-to-last story, "The Poor and Burning Arab," along with the figures Uncle Melik, Uncle Zorab, and Uncle Gyko, do lend continuity to the book, but not enough to support the claim made on the book jacket that the stories "achieve the unity of a novel." One might say the same of Hinojosa's novels. For example, in *Klail City*, within the first twenty-five pages, Hinojosa includes the following sections: "Time Marked and Time Bided," a sort of mock-prologue; "The Tamez Family," an account of an illegitimate pregnancy and the resulting wedding; "Echevarría Has the Floor—Choche Markham: A Cantina Monologue," in which Echevarría cuts loose on the scoundrel; "Doña Sóstenes," in which Rafe recounts one of Echevarría's finer moments; and "The Buenrostro-Leguizamón Affair," in which Rafe is told about the old feuds.

In *Korean Love Songs*, which, along with *The Useless Servants*, is the real genesis of the *Klail City Death Trip Series*, Hinojosa focuses on the personal, the daily flux of war, the moves, the cinemascope of changing scenes, and the ultimate psychical detachment of the individual in the face of rapid and often devastating change. What we see in *Korean Love Songs* and *The Useless Servants* is Rafe's account of his motley life in the armed forces. As Robert Morris says, "the novel that would emphasize character and theme over idea or action must never allow an incident of history to exceed in scope or brilliance a character's perception of it" (xvi). Certainly Hinojosa does not allow the war to supersede Rafe's perception of it. Instead, Rafe writes not only "what happened," an absolute necessity in a genre such as the journal or diary, but he also reveals what he and his fellow soldiers felt or thought or said. The emphasis, despite the drama of battle, is always on the human response.

Though Hinojosa's work does not develop character in the usual way, he is himself more interested in character and theme than in plot—he has openly disavowed any faith in plot to help him fulfill his fictional aims ("Sense of Place" 21). Because *Korean Love Songs* and *The Useless Servants* are both essentially journals kept by Rafe during the war, what we see of the Korean War, or of war in the generic sense, is Rafe's personal perception of it. In *Korean Love Songs*, it is sometimes Rafe's voice, sometimes the voices of his comrades, sometimes voices of the living speaking from hell. In *The Useless Servants*, Rafe's voice as he loses his innocence, and in many ways his youth, ranges from bemusement to outrage to pain. Rafe's changing tone of voice reflects the change he is undergoing and thus transforms the cold, impersonal term "war" to an immediate individual human experience.

Throughout the *Death Trip Series* it is a character's perception of an event that strikes the significant note for Hinojosa. As he has said of *The Valley*, in reference to Baldemar Cordero, who has been accused of stabbing Ernesto Tamez, "I wanted a first-person perspective by Balde, and by the other characters as well" (J. D. Saldívar, "Our Southwest" 184). The dramatic event—the moments leading up to the murder and the murder itself—is never, to use Robert Morris's term, "onstage."

Hinojosa relies on this technique again and again, just as Robert Morris claims the writer of the novel sequence often will. In *Becky and Her Friends*, the last chronological book of the series, Hinojosa takes this method to its potential limit, as he allows Becky's "friends" (a sometimes ironic term) to speak about her actions. The events these characters comment on are never dramatized—they happened entirely in the past.

---

[1] See Alan Warren Friedman's *Multivalence: The Moral Quality of Form in the Modern Novel*. Friedman's study contains an appendix (pp.185–97) entitled "A Galaxy of Multivolume Narration" which catalogs novels under subheadings like "Participant Narration," "Multiple Character Narration," "Several Protagonists," "Family/Social Chronicle," etc. This compendium suggests that Hinojosa's *Death Trip* is a part of a flourishing tradition dating back to Homer.

[2] Catherine Agrella, on the other hand, says *Becky* alone is "a serial melodrama" (review of *Becky and Her Friends*, *Dallas Morning News*, 25 Nov. 1990, J7).

[3] This is in contrast to Rafe's comment when he begins teaching at Klail High with two of his old classmates: "I couldn't stand them back then and I still can't. It's better that way; takes the hypocrisy out of it" (*Claros Varones* 50).

[4] See Mark Busby, "Faulkerian Elements in Rolando Hinojosa's *The Valley*." This is an exellent comparison of both content and style.

4

"Lying to
with Sails Set"
The Trip Begins

Rolando Hinojosa at-
tempts a great deal in his earliest novels, and in large
part, he succeeds. Using a "vaguely elegiac" tone, he
creates a realistic sense of a time, a place, and a people
(Randolph, "Death's" 40). He achieves some remark-
ably vivid dialogue, monologue, and narrative. He
borrows from an old folk form, the *corrido*, and per-
forms some clever manipulations upon it, revealing
at the same time his reliance on modernist techniques. Further, he shows the racism of the Río

Grande Valley without condemning all Anglos to stereotypical treatment.[1]

While Hinojosa does not reveal himself to be a
radical or a political revolutionary in describing the
life of the Mexican-American community generally
and the conditions of migrant life particularly, he does
not shrink from depicting the hardship and injustice
suffered by *mejicanos*. Although he depicts them artistically, rather than ideologically, such material cannot help but be seen as "political," for it reveals the
plight of the ethnic minority.

The action of Rolando Hinojosa's first books is
set for the most part in the 1930s and 1940s, although
he moves forward and backward in time with ease,
from the nineteenth century to the 1970s. Rosaura
Sánchez has pointed out that in the novels up to *Dear
Rafe*, *Partners in Crime*, and *Becky and her Friends*,
the books of the *Klail City Death Trip* sequence "are
narrated from the perspective of the decade of the
seventies as the narrators look back to the thirties,
forties, and fifties and even beyond, to the early part
of the twentieth century" (77). In the early works,
published in the seventies, Hinojosa relies heavily on
the past to help establish a sense of place and to reveal a history which appears more dignified, coherent, and meaningful than the present.

He relies on much of the same material in *Claros
Varones de Belken*, but the real interest of that work

is that it fills in some gaps in the lives of Jehú and Rafe—one learns that they both enlisted in the army and were called to service in Korea, where they spent about thirty months; they returned to Klail City, where Rafe did odd jobs and Jehú first taught English at Klail High (*Klail City* 141) and then worked at the local bank. Then, after three years or so, they went to the University of Texas at Austin. Upon graduation, they both began teaching at Klail City High. Ultimately, Jehú returns to the bank and Rafe gets a law degree. One also learns that Rafe is a widower.

Except for the sections of *Klail City* that recount Rafe's days in the American school and a few scenes in *Claros Varones de Belken*, not until *Dear Rafe*, set after the Korean War, does Hinojosa introduce a serious concern with racial issues.[2] His primary focus in the novels about the pre-war Valley here is on the community's function as a strong, unified entity, although in several sections of *Klail City* and *Claros Varones de Belken*, both of which have a darker tone than *The Valley*, a genuine sense of outrage exists about the racial inequality that shapes the relationship between the Anglos and the Mexicans. In the early installments of the series such overt, explicit treatment of racial inequity only occasionally dominates and is always tempered by the existence of a pre-war *mejicano* sense of community that is both discrete and coherent.

Later, the coherence of the community is tested by outside pressures. The Anglos prevail in the region, and the *mejicanos* are forced to adjust to the Anglo way, or, as don Aureliano puts it, to educate themselves in "the ways of the Romans" (*Klail City* 39). As the *Death Trip Series* progresses, Hinojosa tries to allow characters to move into the Anglo world without sacrificing too much that is unique to their own heritage, a difficult if not impossible balance to achieve.

Rosaura Sánchez recognizes the integrity of Hinojosa's vision of the past in the Mexican-American community of the Valley as she argues for an "idyllic" era that lasted until the mid-twentieth century:

> In these various periods the community faced threats from the outside, from the Anglo world; but apparently it remained largely segregated, a world unto itself, generation after generation. The Mexican Valley remained an idyllic place where the collective spirit reigned amidst heterogeneity. (77)

The *esprit de corps* that Sánchez identifies in the early works is articulated in the first section of *Klail City*, entitled "Time Marked and Time Bided." The narrator says, "Individual and communal heroism calls for patience and forbearance. This makes for a more interesting life, by the way" (10). This idea is less visible in later works such as *Claros Varones de Belken*, *Dear Rafe*, *Rites and Witnesses*, *Partners in Crime* and *Becky and Her Friends*, all of which reveal a more splintered, fragmented community undergoing an evolution of attitude that is occasioned by the inevitable march of time.

Sánchez argues that Hinojosa's style, which she correctly identifies as fragmentary and capsulistic, "decontextualizes events so that the impact of history or social change on individual lives and on particular social classes is not evident" (77). José David Saldívar also argues that the character Echevarría, "like Faulkner's and García Márquez's characters" is engaged in "an ideological nostalgia for an idyllic past where 'that Río Grande was there to provide us with water, not as a fence to separate us one from the other.'" Saldívar is of the opinion that "many of Hinojosa's old guard Texas Mexicans want to stop the clock of time" ("Rolando" 50). But Hinojosa is not an ideologue, and his primary aim in the series is to explore the impact of history and social change on individuals *and* the Mexican American community; furthermore, Echevarría is doing more than nostalgically reminiscing: he is an archetypal wise man engaged in storytelling in its original sense—as oral history.

The *Death Trip Series* concerns itself with historical time and social and individual change. The very word "trip" in the title clearly denotes change, an alteration in time and circumstance. P. Galindo in *Klail City*, in the section "Time Marked and Time Bided," reveals the significance of time and change to the development of the sequence:

> Well now, some of the taxpayers to be seen in Klail City have appeared on other occasions and at other times; in times past, some have scarcely been mentioned at all, and then, of course, there are those who are coming out for the first time; making their debut, as it were. (9)

Robert Morris claims in his book *Continuance and Change* that any sequence novel is necessarily concerned with change (xiii). Hinojosa, moving as he does from past to present, delineates the movement of the major characters from that insular pre-war Mexican culture into the broader, more complicated world. Individual characters must integrate the familiar experience of the old culture with the new experience of the Anglo culture. The epigraph of his first novel,

The Valley, explains what the "trip" of the sequence must accomplish when Hinojosa cites Matthew Arnold's famous lines from "Stanzas from the Grand Chartreuse" about being "between two worlds." The "trip" of the *Death Trip* sequence is a trip from one culture to another; it is a bridge—at the same time that it is a process—between one time period in history and another.[3]

In the pre-war novels, Hinojosa creates a dynamic, vital community without providing vivid physical descriptions of either characters or setting. It is as though Hinojosa introduced a cast of a thousand "extras" in the early works, only to see the stars emerge in the later ones. The atmosphere of the early works is at once comic and tragic, ironic and ingenuous. Hinojosa has commented on his use of humor and irony, saying that for a variety of personal reasons, "humor creeps into my writing once in a while, because it was the use of irony, as many of us know, that allowed the Borderer to survive and maintain a certain measure of dignity" ("Sense of Place" 24). Hinojosa fails to mention in that essay that a tragic irony may also be found in his work as he creates a multilayered atmosphere which shifts rapidly from irony to humor to pathos to tragedy.

Though Hinojosa tries to sustain this atmosphere throughout the novels of the *Klail City Death Trip Series*, some of the later works lack the vitality of

The Valley, *Generaciones*, and *Klail City*. One reason
is that the irony turns almost entirely to pedestrian
earnestness, particularly in *Partners* and *Becky*.
Rosaura Sánchez has explained the difference between the early works and some of the later ones as a
result of what she sees as a "politicizing" trend in the
progress of the sequence. She says the first two books
(*The Valley* and *Generaciones y Semblanzas*), deal only
with "heterogeneity in the community," while the others "explore the social and class contradictions in the
Valley" (76). The odd man out here is *Claros Varones
de Belken*. Though written fairly early in the
sequence—the fourth book, after *Estampas*,
Generaciones y Semblanzas, and *Generaciones, Notas
y Brechas*—it deals with both the early community
(though much of the material is repeated from the
earlier works), *and* it shows Jehú and Rafe after their
time in Korea and while they are students together
at the University of Texas. So it shows both the old
coherence and the increasing fragmentation of tradition in a single novel.

Despite what a number of Chicano critics say,
none of these works shows Hinojosa becoming more
political as he continues the sequence. In fact, he has
argued consistently in speeches, interviews, and essays that he does not intend to take a political stance.
He emphasizes that "didacticism, totalitarian themes,
boxed-in theses, and set propositions are intolerable

and inexcusable for the serious writer of fiction and
nonfiction, or of criticism for that matter" (Bruce-
Novoa, "Rolando" 53). What happens in the later
works seems less a political conversion (in the sense
of a new concern for the fact of discrimination) than
it does a simple recognition of change. The move toward assimilation prevents an exclusive concern with
the old community. And Hinojosa clearly sees that
the passage of time—history—is precipitating that
move toward assimilation.

I do not mean to suggest that Hinojosa is unaware
of discrimination and the often untenable position of
the Mexican American, because in spite of his focus
on a coherent community in the pre-war novels
Hinojosa does write about outside discrimination in
these early works, such as his description of the death
of Ambrosia Mora, a World War II veteran shot in the
back by an Anglo policeman who goes unpunished.
Hinojosa knows that racism is a historical fact, and
he does not shrink from showing it. But his novels
also show that in the post-World War II era the
mejicano community feels empowered and so cannot
continue to respond to racism (as well as many other
issues) in the old ways.

Nevertheless, the overall tone of the first novels,
even when they deal with racism and other sorts of
human misery, is often one of nostalgic innocence,
combined with a true zest for life in all its manifesta-

tions. For example, in *The Valley*, the brief monologues
of Tere and Roque Malacara, Jehú's parents, are characterized by a depth of emotion that would not be
found in a work characterized *only* by irony and humor. The voice of Tere is at once tragic and ingenuous when she says, "Now, if I were educated I'd be
able to say this much better, wouldn't I? Finer, maybe,
but the trouble is, I'm just plain tired" (13). Yet the
voice is also ironic and humorous as she comments
on the perils of working as a housekeeper: "I mean,
there's the Mister and the Mister's son, and (I know
what I'm talking about) it's best to keep an eye on the
Mrs. herself, you bet" (13). The pathos in her voice as
she comments on her physical condition is only fully
revealed in the succeeding monologue of her husband:
"Tere's my wife, and I know she's tired. S'got every
right to be so. We only have the boy now; Tere and I
have seen to the burial of my father-in-law and our
three girls" (14).

In another telling example of Hinojosa's ability
to blend humor, pathos, irony, and the frankness of a
"folk" culture, Jehú and other family members respond to the death of his father, Roque, which occurs
two years after the death of Tere Malacara. Jehú is
nine years old when Roque dies, but tells the story as
an adult. The voice in "Lying to with Sails Set," and
"About Those Relatives of Mine" has something of the
precocious and knowing yet paradoxically innocent

child about it, even though it is "twenty-five years and two wars later" when Jehú speaks of these events (15). Ostensibly, the voice of Jehú in *Rites and Witnesses* is chronologically the same voice heard in *The Valley*, even though the tone in *The Valley* is much less sophisticated and urbane than the one in *Rites and Witnesses*.

In *The Valley*, Jehú remembers that his father died one day, "just like that" (15) as he was telling Jehú a joke. This ironic juxtaposition of the joke and the death is typical Hinojosa, but as Jehú recounts the day, he does not seem to see the irony; instead, he rather naively goes on to say that the day his father died was the day that "a knockabout carny troupe" (15) arrived in his hometown of Relampago, an important fact since Jehú ends up leaving town with the troupe. Yet Jehú's apparent innocence of the black humor attending the circumstance of his father's death is also typical Hinojosa. Bruce-Novoa calls this characteristic of Hinojosa's fiction "a persistent and welcome understatement" (50), and here as elsewhere it helps to sustain an emotionally rich atmosphere that is never marred by sentimentality or excess of any kind.

Another example of Hinojosa's ability to avoid sentimentality when evoking the past is found in scenes of Aunt Chedes's "trances" in *The Valley*. At the end of the chapter "Lying to with Sails Set," Aunt

Chedes interrupts her ironing to perform a ritual for
the orphaned Jehú. She places her middle finger—
"all of it, to the hilt"—in her mouth, then in a glass of
cold water, after which she makes the sign of the cross
in the air and on Jehú's forehead. She tells him to
drink the water without stopping as she says an "Our
Father" backwards, since "today's the day you're to
meet your new Pa" (16). Jehú's skeptical response is
an early clue to his adult personality, though his comment is rather tongue-in-cheek:

> I looked at her, but she wouldn't start until I
> started to drink. Standing there, mouth
> agape, I didn't know what to do, but—just in
> case—'cause you never can tell, I took the
> glass and began to drink as she half-
> hummed, half-sung out: Amen, evil from us
> deliver and . . . . (17)

Aunt Chedes's earnestness and Jehú's skepticism create the humor in the situation arising from the death
of Jehú's father, which makes Jehú an orphan and is
no laughing matter. Yet Hinojosa manages to make
us smile at Jehú's circumstances. Jehú has had the
world open up before him, paradoxically through the
death of his father. Like Huck, he is now a pilgrim,
and he takes to the road with a carny troupe. Jehú is
now living in a world of possibility, with the romance

of the open road awaiting him. It is interesting to note when considering the Janus-face of Hinojosa's main characters that Rafe Buenrostro is also orphaned at an early age.

Maintaining a sense of a coherent community is not a problem for Hinojosa in *The Valley* or *Klail City*. Despite his fragmented style, there seems to be a clear ethos among the members of the community. One of Hinojosa's techniques for revealing this spirit of community is to borrow from the folk culture a form called the *corrido*, a type of ballad about the struggle against oppression which Luis Leal describes as "a typical poetic form of the Mexican populace." Leal says that this literary form can be traced to what he terms the "Hispanic Period," which lasted from colonization to 1821, and that it has served as a "primary vehicle toward self-understanding and self-definition" (23). Hinojosa has used the *corrido* within the larger framework of his novels as a vehicle for defining the Mexican-American community, as well as for documenting social protest. By using and manipulating his version of the *corrido*, Hinojosa is able to present some of the bleaker aspects of life, such as the hardships of farm workers, and simply man's inhumanity to man. He also uses a variation on the *corrido* form to reveal the significance of the surrogate author P. Galindo to the development of the series. The *corrido* as it appears in Hinojosa's work is not an exclusive and docu-

mentary internal device used solely for the self-edifi-
cation of the Mexican-American community, but is
transformed instead into an artistic device to further
the aims of his sequence novel.

Hinojosa uses variations of two typical subjects
of the *corrido* in *The Valley* and *Klail City*. According
to Américo Paredes, the *corrido*, whatever its origin,
is often concerned with "a Mexican whose rights or
self-respect are trampled upon by North American
authority" or "a group of Mexicans whose work forces
them to travel deep into the United States" ("The Folk
Base" 13). In the first instance, revenge is a traditional motif: the hero is usually avenging the "cruel
and unjust" death of his brother "at the hands of
Anglo-Americans." Outnumbered by Texas Rangers
or "rinches," the hero is viciously set upon ("The Folk
Base" 13). Hinojosa uses a variant of this motif in the
account of Ambrosio Mora's death. First told in
Generaciones, and also appearing in *Klail City* in the
section entitled, "The Older Generation II," the story
of how Mora is "shot down by Van Meers in front of
the J.C. Penney in downtown Flora on a Palm Sun-
day afternoon" is clearly in the tradition of the *corrido*,
yet it also borrows from the modernist idea of the
impotent hero. The narrator's account is more than
reportorial. Van Meers is acquitted, after a three-year
delay of the trial, and though "there was a lot of noise
and commotion" from the Mexican-American commu-

nity, "nothing came of it" (*Generaciones* 148). Yet
Ambrosio's death *is* avenged, not by a brother, but by
his father, who had lost yet another son in the war:

> Don Aureliano himself went out to the band-
> stand in the Klail City park with a crowbar
> in hand. He smashed the metal plaque that
> bore the names of all the Klail men who had
> served during the war, among them Ambrosio
> and the other son, Amador, who died in
> Okinawa. Don Aureliano completely demol-
> ished the plaque donated by the Ladies Aux-
> iliary of the American Legion. The whole
> thing was reduced to a pile of rubbish.
> (*Generaciones* 148)

Don Aureliano's revenge is little more than symbolic,
but it does conform to the conventions of the *corrido*
in that the unjust death is in one way or another
avenged, and as a sort of echo of this *corrido*, the community creates a ballad about the death of Ambrosio
Mora. But both this symbolic revenge and the personal revenge that don Aureliano intends to have by
outliving Van Meers reveal Hinojosa's modernist ori-
entation, the attitude that the hero suffers an inabil-
ity to alter circumstances or act effectively. Don
Aureliano is a sad and angry old man, not the young,
strong hero of the traditional *corrido*. Unable to

change things, he can only vent his emotions by destroying a plaque. When he says the *mejicanos* are "Greeks in the land of the Romans," don Aureliano recognizes that he is living in a world where he has little power, and that even an act of heroism is necessarily diminished by the absurdity of the "codes," written or unwritten, of that world (*Generaciones* 148). He says the Romans have to be educated, but assumes that it cannot happen. He laments the *mejicanos'* loss of control over their own lives, saying, "the day will come when *la raza* will live in Belken County like it did before these bastards came here" (*Generaciones* 150). Of course, in that earlier time, it was not called "Belken County," and, sadly, historical change is documented and in a sense validated by his articulation of those two words alone.

Still, don Aureliano *is,* for the narrator, a hero, suggesting a type of heroism that consists primarily of endurance: "The sign incident happened over twenty years ago and if *la raza* didn't end up educating the Romans like the Greeks did, at least we thrived like grapes: in bunches." Furthermore, don Aureliano has perseverance: "He's a quarter-of-a-century older than Van Meers, but he has all the patience in the world and plans to attend the funeral of his son's killer in person . . . . don Aureliano will not be sent tumbling down by any breeze nor by the years until he attends Van Meers' funeral. I swear to God" (*Generaciones* 148, 150). This modernist perception of heroism as persistence and endurance is also found in the opening sections of *Klail City*, when the narrator offers a "caveat" on heroes:

> One shouldn't expect to find legendary heroes here . . . the reader who looks for a hero . . . will be given short shrift. . . . No heroes, then, although the reader knows, senses, suspects that there are certain and definite ways of being heroic. Showing up for work (and doing it) and then putting up with whatever fool comes bobbing along is no laughing matter. (9)

With the exception of some figures from the past—don Julian Buenrostro, and perhaps the young soldier Rafe—Hinojosa maintains this stance on the hero until *Partners in Crime*, in which we can take P. Galindo's voice as the writer's own.[4] Hinojosa's literary stance is modernist, but in these early works, he also relies on older ethnic forms and subject matter, while throughout the series he is influenced by the orality of both modernist writers such as Joyce and of traditional Mexican-American stories, a fact which reveals the duality of his vision as an artist. In addition, as Mark Busby has noted, Hinojosa and Faulkner use similar stylistic devices and rely heavily on "folklore and folk tales" ("Faulknerian" 107).

In other variations on the *corrido*, Hinojosa further reveals his dualism. The death of Rafe Buenrostro's father, Jesús, borrows from the *corrido* in that it is Jesús's brother Julián who avenges his death, which, like the death of the victim in the traditional *corrido*, is "cruel and unjust" (Paredes, "The Folk Base" 13). In *Generaciones*, we find that "One night, in April, when the orange trees were ready to blossom . . . someone came and killed don Jesús while he slept" (22). The sound of don Julián's approaching horse scared the murderer away. Two months later, Julián discovers the names of the guilty, and then goes "into the woods on horseback and across the Río Grande in search of his brother's killers" (22, 24). The murder turns out to have been the result of a land dispute with the Leguizamón family:

> Alejandro Leguizamón had paid two Mexican nationals to kill don Jesús. They probably never had time to enjoy the money because don Julián dispatched them swiftly while his horse was still dripping water from the Río Bravo . . . Alejandro Leguizamón was found in the courtyard of the Sacred Heart Church with his head bashed in. (24)

In this variation, it would seem that Hinojosa has forfeited his typical stance: that endurance not action is the mark of the hero. Or perhaps he sees both as ways of surviving, of being heroic. Don Julián certainly qualifies as a traditional hero. In any case, Hinojosa has not abandoned his dual vision, for here we see the Mexican American to be just as capable of evil deeds as the Anglo. It is perhaps fictional incidents such as this one that have led Hinojosa to note that "some say [my work] isn't political—maybe they mean not political enough. . . . Some well-meaning people fret that Anglos may not receive a good impression of us" (Bruce-Novoa, "Rolando" 56, 61). As Hinojosa says, some Chicano writers won't or can't "present the verities" of Chicano life, "rural, urban, young, old, good, bad, sick, well, at home, at work, in love . . ." (Bruce-Novoa, "Rolando" 61). Hinojosa presents the "verities" of life in the *mejicano* community as he shows the sharp practices and murders that take place among Mexican Americans. In addition to Hinojosa's picture of the *coyotes*, those Chicanos who prey upon their own people, he depicts darker conflicts within the Mexican-American community. One example is the murder of Ernesto Tamez, who torments and is then killed by Baldemar Cordero at the *Aquí mi quedo* cantina. "The Tamezes are a peculiar bunch of people . . . they were forever into something with someone, the neighbors, anybody" (*The Valley*

64). That Ernesto Tamez is Mexican American, like
the scheming Lequizamóns, does not destroy for
Hinojosa the integrity of the Mexican-American community. Just as the same things happen to different
people at different times in history ("Sense of Place"
24), for Hinojosa the same types of people appear
within all racial groups.

Interestingly, the Tamez-Cordero incident can be
seen as another variation on the *corrido*. Luis Leal
has written of a particular *corrido* as being significant because it "introduces the theme of social protest" (26). Though Leal writes of a particular ballad
that deals specifically with Anglo-Mexican conflict,
clear parallels exist between it and the situation of
Baldemar Cordero, and like the *corrido* Leal speaks
of, the Cordero incident can ultimately be seen as a
form of social protest. The *corridista* Leal mentions
complains that justice has not been served:

> Thirty-three days in jail
> unjustly I have suffered
> because of a false witness
> of a crime I did not commit
> When the judge handed down his sentence
> it almost made me laugh—
> the guilty one would go free
> while the innocent was left to suffer. (26)

The main point of these lines is that someone is being punished for a crime he did not commit. In the case of Baldemar Cordero, it is clear that he has not, from the narrator's point of view, committed a "crime" in the usual sense. He has been goaded into spontaneous action by the repeated taunts and tricks of Ernesto Tamez. Cordero acts without thought, without a moment's premeditation, and with just provocation. Yet there are witnesses to the scene; it cannot be denied that Cordero stabbed Tamez—even Cordero does not deny it. But the eyewitness accounts of the incident cannot adequately explain what happened, at least not sufficiently to keep Cordero from being found guilty. (This incident is a kind of metaphor for the entire series—events, history, life itself cannot be adequately explained, no matter how many versions are presented.)

An excerpt from *The Klail City Enterprise-News* reveals that Cordero was sent to Huntsville for fifteen years. The narrator clearly finds Cordero's sentencing an absurd miscarriage of "justice" (*The Valley* 70). In the newspaper account of the sentencing, the syntax is garbled, the murder victim's name is misspelled, and, most important, the reasons for the murder are neatly and incorrectly summed up in a single statement:

Klail City. (Special). Baldemar Cordero, 30,
of 169 South Hidalgo Street, drew a 15 year
sentence Harrison Pehelp's 139th District
Court, for the to the Huntsville Judge in State
Prison murder of Ernesto Tamez, also 30,
over the affections of one of the "hostesses"
who works there. ETAOIN SHRUDLU PICK
UP No appeal had been made at press time.
(70)

Since this incident involves only Mexican Americans,
including Cordero's lawyer, Romeo Hinojosa, the
mangling of the news story can be seen as commentary on the Anglo establishment's lack of interest in
the "doings" of the Mexican-American community.
This fact is mentioned by Rafe in *The Valley*:

The bald truth is that our fellow Texans
across the tracks could hardly care about
what we think, say, or do. . . . Here's something of what the A.T.s usually say: "Oh, it's
nothing, really; just one of your usual Mexican cantina fan-dan-goes 's all. They drink a
little beer, they play them rancheras on the
juke box, don't you know; and then one o'
them lets out a big squeal, and the first thing
you know, why, they's having theirselves a
fight." (51)

The Baldero Cordero incident, like the *corrido* Leal mentions, is clearly social protest. It may be that the trial adhered to all the technical legalities, but it is also evident that the truth has been subverted and that justice has not been served in the case of Baldero Cordero or the community in general.

Since the *corrido* lends itself particularly to social protest, Hinojosa uses the form a number of times in the series, especially when depicting the plight of the migrant workers. Paredes describes the migrant *corrido* as being about

> a group of Mexicans whose work forces them to travel deep into the United States. Always narrated in the first person plural, these *corridos* recount the perils of the trip, the foreign cities, and the strange things seen by the adventurers. ("The Folk Base" 13)

In *The Valley* and *Klail City* we see variations on this form of the *corrido* in a number of places (although never told in the first person plural), but most particularly in the sections of *Klail City* entitled, "The Searchers." P. Galindo, the narrator, recounts trips with Leocadio Gavira, the owner of the truck named *Oklahoma Fireball Express* that carries the migrant workers north. On the first day, the truck stops in

Rosenberg, Texas, and P. Galindo ponders the people and the trip they are making:

> The Okla. Fireball was half way to Texarkana that first day; the people, *la gente*, were all from Belken County—Klail City, Bascom, Flora, and Edgerton—and on their way to Benton Harbor and St. Joseph to work the Welch grape vineyards near Lake Michigan. (*Klail City* 62)

In the five sections that make up "The Searchers" in *Klail City*, P. Galindo recounts the situation of the people who decide to make the trip and presents their preparations for the trip as an integral part of the journey itself. He also includes conversations that take place between himself and Gavira. One of the most poignant "adventures" depicts the death of Señor and Señora Esteban in an auto accident and the efforts of their daughter and son-in-law to get their bodies back to Texas. When her parents are killed en route to northern Colorado, Claudia Rivas and her husband, Teodoro, are "on the migrant trail to Mankato, Minnesota" (*Klail City* 67). Once the bodies are identified, the "town pharmacist-coroner-undertaker notifies the Texas dependents by phone; they then call the migrant labor camp in Tulsa, Oklahoma, where the Rivas couple has stopped for the night" (*Klail City* 67). The younger couple encounters both greedy and helpful Anglos. The Justice of the Peace, "Old Man Fikes," takes them for twenty dollars for the death certificates, but the pharmacist who receives the bodies is kind to the young people and readily agrees to let them send him payment later. The Rivases then set out for Sedalia, Missouri, to meet up with some other Texans, who are looking after their children. Their life on the road and their life in the Valley are inseparable.

Although Hinojosa's focus in the *Death Trip* sequence cannot be called agricultural, and he has said that it is naive and provincial to say that Chicano literature is inherently agricultural (Bruce-Novoa, "Rolando" 58), these sections of *Klail City* deal directly with the fact of migrant labor in the Mexican-American community. And even though Rosaura Sánchez has argued that Hinojosa rarely presents his characters at work, but instead focuses on their personal lives, in these sections of *Klail City* the characters' personal lives are shown to hinge directly on the fact of their particular type of employment (79). Hinojosa also shows the immediate conditions that force some of these families into the migrant labor force:

> It's August in Belken County, and the cotton pickings are slim since the third pick's been done with. The citrus crop . . . is still some

four months away; December the earliest....
So there's nothing to do but go Up North.
Take one's chances on the road up and back,
1500 mi., each way. A bitch. (*Klail City* 50)

The speaker then offers the opinion that the people
have no choice: "We can stay here and eat shit till
December" (50). The hasty preparations for the trip
are recounted as voices call to one another: "Who you
leaving your house keys with?" and "What about the
kids' schooling?" These questions must be settled,
along with the problem of finding drivers and fixing
contracts. The workers fear that if the contracts are
not completed before they leave they will be forced to
stay up north until January and February, after the
orange harvest in the Valley has already begun (*Klail
City* 50–53).

Hinojosa freely manipulates the *corrido* theme
when P. Galindo identifies himself as "the writer"
(*Klail City* 55). He says his trips with Leocadio Gavira
were "made in good faith" and that he "managed to
pull his load" by driving, changing tires, and staying
out of people's way. The identification of P. Galindo
as "the writer," and hence with Hinojosa, provides a
significant variation on the form of the *corrido*. The
subject matter is essentially in line with Paredes's
description, but the inclusion of P. Galindo's commen-

tary and perspective makes this story of migrant
workers more than a simple oral retelling of events
meant to bond members of a community together.
Much of what he says is strikingly similar to statements that Hinojosa has made elsewhere, about both
himself and life in general.

Before he begins recounting the trip, Galindo
explains his reasons for going along:

> The writer wanted to remember certain
> people and make sure that these people were
> remembered in writing. The writer is con-
> vinced that he did well not to have written
> about the trips on the spot; he believes in
> Time, that leveler he spoke of. (55)

In an essay called "A Voice of One's Own," Hinojosa
says of his qualifications as a writer and critic that
"time will take care of that piece of business. Time is
the ultimate judge. . . . Time is also the great leveler"
("Sense of Place" 15). Hinojosa's own comments about
why he decided to write about the Valley echo these
statements of P. Galindo's, particularly his statement
that he wished always to present his parents faith-
fully and not to write about "their mutual cultures as
if they were pieces of some half-baked mosaic" ("Sense
of Place" 14). The body of work itself suggests that he

wants to "make sure that these people were remembered in writing" (*Klail City* 55).

Even more convincing evidence that P. Galindo is "perhaps an alter ego of Hinojosa himself" (José David Saldívar, *The Dialectics of Our America* 75), are several confessional statements made by Hinojosa in various places, especially when they are considered in the light of P. Galindo's comments in *Klail City* on the sort of life he has led:

> The writer worked in some very odd jobs and for some very odd people for the first thirty years of his life. . . . In the course of that time, schooling of all forms and shapes interfered as well, as did some personal events. . . . Those odd jobs and odder people referred to earlier caused the writer to change his style of life for a while, but this proved to be temporary. But, it was also beneficial: the writer needed that experience too . . . [he] now feels he's back on track, having recovered, ransomed perhaps, the knowledge of who he was and where he came from. . . . the writer—if he is nothing else—thinks himself quite lucky and fortunate, too, to have recovered a part of his life that he'd almost forgotten, that he had, insensibly, unthinkingly, turned his back on. (*Klail City* 57)

In this long passage, P. Galindo reveals a great deal about Rolando Hinojosa. Hinojosa has said, "It is the time of my childhood and young manhood that have served me well in my writing; that, and a somewhat sketchy education, [and] an interestingly remarkable homelife" ("Sense of Place" 17). He has also noted that he was able to write in part because of luck—because of who he is and where he comes from, coupled with "the proper historical moment." The moment, he says,

> came along and I took what had been there for some time, but which I had not been able to see, since I had not fully developed a sense of place; I had left the Valley for the service, for formal university training, and for a series of very odd jobs, only to return to it in my writing. ("Sense of Place" 23–24)

Hinojosa further clarifies that he and P. Galindo "come from the same place" by saying that "values and decisions" are "inculcated by one's elders first, by one's acquaintances later on . . . [and] one's place of origin" ("Sense of Place" 24). He speaks of the decision to write and then trying to decide what to write about. What may be most important to the writer is a kind of "preparatory stage," experience that helps one write about something "when time presents itself" ("Sense of Place" 24).

Without straining too much, it is easy to see that
P. Galindo's confession, or perhaps more properly, his
manifesto, tells the story of Hinojosa's evolution as a
writer, as revealed by his comment that "What I
worked on, as far as my life was concerned, was toward a personal voice which was to become my public voice" ("A Voice of One's Own" 13). These personal
and public voices speak in harmony particularly in
The Valley, *Klail City*, and in parts of other novels
containing reminiscences of this period. Hinojosa is
describing a world literally—a world he knew intimately and of which he was an undisputed member.
His persona is coherent. He knows who he is and
where he fits in, even if the specter of racial inequality lurks just outside the perimeters of his world. This
is the situation of the well-adjusted child, and as it
was with Jehú Malacara and Rafe Buenrostro, so it
was with Rolando Hinojosa.

In spite of the racial tension which is accelerated
as the young boys move into the Anglo world—at first
into the Anglo schools—they know who they are. As
they notice the differences between the North Ward
mejicanos and the South Ward mejicanos, they reveal how they see themselves. The South Ward
mejicanos, called "the dispossessed" by Jehú, "were
one hell of a lot more fluent in English than we were"
(*Klail City* 70), but they appear to have been put in

their place and to be willing to go along with it. As for Rafe and the other South Ward *mejicanos*, they "demanded" their share. They insisted on being treated as equal because it was "the American way" (*Klail City* 70). They knew they were equal and demanded that others recognize it. This basic fact of their character gives them an edge in the competitive games that they later must play. As they grow older, achieving equality becomes both more complex and more important, because the question is no longer who gets good gym equipment, but who gets a "good" life. Even the definition of the good life become harder to pin down. As time, "that great leveler," passes, their world expands, and, finally, collapses. What was whole becomes fragmented.[5] Hinojosa's characters face the tortuous task of trying to piece together a new world for themselves.

Hinojosa successfully treats highly political subjects in a creative way—as an artist rather than as a propagandist. He shows the Mexican American in a variety of manifestations, mostly sympathetic, but with an honesty and candor that often surprises. In short, the early novels demonstrate his integrity as an artist and his grasp of a number of literary and folk techniques as he depicts a coherent community.[6]

---

[1] Manuel M. Martín-Rodríguez has dealt with the shortcomings of the Mexican-American community (as in the case of Ambrosio Mora's murder, the Leguizamóns' double-dealings, Ira Escobar's willingness to be an Anglo pawn, and the *mejicanos'* willingness to believe the worst of Jehú when he leaves the bank) in "El Tema Ya Culpa En Cuatro Novelistas Chicanos."

[2] Serge Ricard argues that a sense of ethnic identity and religion help the Mexican American to survive and points out that Rafe and Jehú's experience in the American school "cruelly" points out the way in which they differ from the Anglos. Yet he goes on to say that the Anglo is a victim as well—a victim of Hinojosa and his characters' humor and irony. Ricard also argues that Hinojosa achieves an "authentic" re-creation of the life of the people in "Un Art de la Survie: Chicanismo et Religion Dans L'oeuvre De Rolando Hinojosa."

[3] See Luis Leal, "History and Memory in *Estampas del Valle*."

[4] Hinojosa's first stories were published under the pseudonym "P. Galindo."

[5] László Scholz argues that both the style of *Klail City* and the community are fragmented. He says Hinojosa's style is like that of Marqúez, Borges, and others who rebel against the "traditional, rounded forms" of the novel, and also that although Hinojosa presents elements that have the potential to create a unified "system" they do not do so in *Klail City*. He says that *Klail City* is neither a full negation nor confirmation of the life of the people. "Fragmentarismo en *Klail City y sus aldredores* de Rolando Hinojosa."

[6] See Heiner Bus's "The Establishment of Community in Zora Neale Hurston's *The Eatonville Anthology* (1926) and Rolando Hinojosa's *Estampas del valle* (1973)."

5

A Change in Direction

Between *Estampas del Valle* and *Becky and Her Friends*, the *Klail City Death Trip Series* moves from life lived in the "old" Valley to life in the "new" Valley. The tone of the novels becomes less "frenetic," (Randolph, "Death's" 40), and the author/narrator becomes more self-aware than he was in the novels of the first period. The pre-war novels depicted a time of stasis in the Mexicano community, but the later novels show a time of dynamic growth and change. The works of the sequence's middle period (*Klail City, Korean Love Songs*, parts of *Claros Varones de Belken, Rites and Witnesses, Dear Rafe*, and *The Useless Servants*) depict alteration and upheaval in the changing world of the early post-

World War II period, the Korean War, and the post-Korean War period. (Later, as I argue in Chapter Six, by the time of *Becky and Her Friends* and *Partners in Crime* the world of the Valley is essentially static again.) In other words, the novels follow the classical pattern of movement from order to chaos and back to order.

Despite the changes depicted during the chaotic middle period the tone of the series loses some of its vitality as Hinojosa's characters move forward in time. Though still compelling, the *Klail City Death Trip Series* becomes a less dynamic but more psychological exploration as it moves from the thirties to the fifties and sixties. *Korean Love Songs* and *The Useless Servants* denote a turning point as Rafe Buenrostro, stripped of all innocence and illusion, contemplates life in the Valley and the spectacle of war. Similarly Jehú Malacara is initiated into the brutality of small-town politics and business. *Rites and Witnesses* alternates between Rafe in Korea and the Anglos who desire to control Jehú as they control Belken County. *Dear Rafe* enlarges the picture of small-town corruption, and *Claros Varones de Belken* fills in some gaps about Rafe's and Jehú's lives as young men, the death of the "storyteller" and "wise man" Estaban Echeverría, and the fragmentation of the Mexican-American community.

José David Saldívar's observation that *"Klail City* projects a world of tragic realism in which the ultimate entanglements of alienation and desire are so anguished as to appear almost beyond salvation" (*Dialectics* 73) is an apt description of this entire "transitional period" in the lives of Hinojosa's major characters. Because this dilemma is also Hinojosa's dilemma, both as a private person and as a public figure, a writer, the autobiographical nature of the *Death Trip* becomes apparent. Both Jehú and Rafe go to college, serve in the armed forces in Korea, and return to college. Rafe, like Hinojosa, majors in Spanish, and Jehú majors in English. They both go beyond the bachelor's degree, though whether Jehú gets a graduate degree is never revealed. Somewhere along the way, Rafe gets a law degree. Jehú's work in the Klail City Bank reflects not only the Valley's parochial economic and social system in those days, but also mirrors Hinojosa's own experience with the bureaucracy as an employee of the Civil Service Commission. Both Rafe and Jehú teach for a time in the local high school, as Hinojosa did in Brownsville. Héctor Torres thinks it is Jehú's "fate to be an alter ego of the one presenting this discourse on the Valley, Hinojosa himself" (88). Donald A. Randolph, in tracing the connection between the character of P. Galindo and Hinojosa, asserts that "there is a great

deal of covert, overt or even semi-concealed autobiography in Hinojosa's works." He argues that "autobiography, both fictional and authentic, has long
persisted as a principal constituent of the main body
of Chicano letters" and goes on to point out the multiple similarities between don Manuel Guzman in the
Death Trip Series and don Manuel G. Hinojosa,
Rolando Hinojosa's father ("Death's" 39). Similarly,
José David Saldívar says, "Rolando Hinojosa's recon-
structed life can serve as a parallel text of the evolution of his literary project" ("Rolando" 44). And Ed
García observes in a 1982 review of *Rites and Witnesses*:

> So far Hinojosa has taken his saga up
> through around 1960, which is about the time
> he finally left the Valley for graduate school.
> . . . [H]is central theme is the changing Val-
> ley and essentially the Anglicization of the
> Mexicans. (26–27)

The artistic danger that lurks just beyond the parameters of such a "fictionalized life" has been aptly
expressed by Leslie Fiedler as he comments on a tendency of the American novelist in general to focus on
"a limited world of experience, usually associated with
his childhood, writing the same book over and over
again until he lapses into silence or self-parody" ("The

Novel" 132). Nevertheless, this autobiographical *Bildungsroman* element is interesting in itself, for it can give fiction a meaning and a depth it would otherwise lack. The idea of the *Bildungsroman* is endlessly fascinating because of the "fifth dimension" that it adds to a work of fiction. As M. M. Bakhtin has noted of any author's position in relation to the work he creates, "he does his observing from his own unresolved and still evolving contemporaneity" (255). Bakhtin's theoretical stance, however, would deny any factual relationship (chronological or spatial) between the author and the created text:

> Even had he created an autobiography or a confession of the most astonishing truthfulness, all the same he, as its creator, remains outside the world he has represented in his work. If I relate (or write about) an event that has just happened to me, then I as the teller (or writer) of this event am already outside the time and space in which the event occurred. It is just as impossible to forge an identity between myself, my own "I," and that "I" that is the subject of my stories as it is to lift myself up by my own hair. (256)

Bakhtin says that to "confuse the author-creator of a work with the author as a human being" is a major failing of criticism of the novel, a methodological weakness he calls "naive biographism" (253). He goes on to argue that "everything becomes an image in the literary work" and thus "is a created thing" (256). He says that a reader usually "creates an image" of the author, but of course it must be acknowledged that the author may just as well "create an image" of himself within a fiction. This is exactly what Hinojosa is doing in the *Klail City Death Trip Series*: creating an image of himself through several surrogate authors.

Though Bakhtin is correct that the "image" of the "I" (whatever person it takes) is *not* the author and perhaps can have no verifiable or documentable relation to him, the created "I" can be a version of the author trying to move toward a personal or artistic resolution. Bakhtin notes the author's perpetually unfinished state, and interestingly, Hinojosa says that in spite of his rich background and career, he is an unfinished product ("A Voice of One's Own" 14). An author's use of autobiography, even altered or embellished autobiography, enables him to produce, not himself, but an image of himself, which he may perceive to be valid and integrated with his non-created self, that is, with the self that exists in real time and space. Bakhtin argues that the reader's created image of the author may be "deep and truthful," in which case "it can help the reader more correctly and pro-

foundly to understand the work of the given author"
(257). Similarly, the author's created image of himself may help him "more correctly and profoundly" to
understand himself. Hinojosa says that although the
"original facts of one's formation" cannot be altered,
"one may mythicize, adopt a persona, become an ac-
tor, restructure family history" ("Sense of Place" 22).
The quest for self-knowledge is a component of what
Bakhtin calls "an enduring chronotope of the novel,"
or "the metaphor of the road, life's course" (244). And
this quest can involve the author as well as the reader.
Obviously the title the *Klail City Death Trip Series*
reveals his awareness of this motif in his own work.

Bakhtin's arguments are significant because they
raise the familiar yet difficult questions about life and
art, questions about which it is easy to be dogmatic
in theory, but which become hard to resolve when one
is faced with something like Hinojosa's *Death Trip*,
where the lines between fact and imagination, history and fiction, reality and individual perception are
undeniably vague. Jill Johnston has argued that "the
quest for a story is a quest for a life," that "writing
and self-creation are synonymous" (29). What Robert Morris says of Anthony Powell's sequence novel,
A Dance to the Music of Time, applies as well to
Hinojosa's *Death Trip*: "In a work that sets out to be
both life and fiction, history and myth, Powell strikes
a balance between what has really happened in the

last fifty years and how the novelist might view its happening" (125).

Hinojosa's *Death Trip*, a sequence novel, also exhibits characteristic features of "the reflexive novel." In his book *The Reflexive Novel*,[1] Michael Boyd says that the writer of such a fiction sees "that the relationship between reality and its representation in fictional discourse is problematical," and in response may write a novel that "seeks to examine the act of writing itself" (7), which is something that P. Galindo in particular seems to be engaged in. Hinojosa, in a similar vein, says of the act of writing, "sometimes it is . . . easier than examining one's conscience" (*Claros Varones* 12). Though Hinojosa is not self-consciously producing reflexive works of the sort analyzed by Boyd, much of what Boyd says about James Joyce, Virginia Woolf, and William Faulkner is helpful in understanding Hinojosa's aims and methods. His use of autobiography mirrors Joyce's. His erratic shifts in point of view can be understood in light of Boyd's argument about Woolf's use of the soliloquy in *The Waves*. And Boyd's analysis of how Faulkner actually makes use of history in *Absalom, Absalom!* (though John Dos Passos's *USA* is just as likely an influence) explains in part Hinojosa's heavy reliance on "documents" such as letters, diaries, depositions, and newspaper reports in recounting events. The similarities between Hinojosa and these other modernists help not only to clarify his fiction, but also to clarify his philosophical and categorical "place" as a proponent of literary modernism.

Ever since Joyce and Woolf began experimenting with the form of the novel, lesser novelists have borrowed their techniques, sometimes because they lacked the technical skills to produce a "traditional" novel. The results, of course, were like the nonrepresentational painting produced by an amateur with no knowledge of perspective—a far different thing from, say, a work by Jackson Pollock or Helen Frankenthaler. One might accuse Hinojosa of the amateur painter's fault, for he does have trouble sustaining a traditional plot, as the novel *Partners in Crime* shows. Louis Dubose, in a review of *Dear Rafe,* asks:

> Are we being strung along for yet another novel of nouvelle length and novel, that is, innovative, narrative style? Or is it that these narrative devices, fragments, personal letters, interviews, depositions, and sketches cannot be sustained long enough to complete one fat *novel* on the Valley? (16)

The fact is that Hinojosa does borrow freely from the typically disjointed "modernist" form of the novel, most often quite successfully. But there is more to his form than mere borrowing of modernist fictional techniques. The similarities between his method in *Korean Love Songs*, *Rites and Witnesses*, *Dear Rafe*, and *Claros Varones* and the work of Joyce and Woolf go beyond this disjointed form to explain some of the problems of point of view in the *Death Trip* sequence. Hinojosa presents a variety of points of view in his work, ostensibly allowing any number of individuals to speak, and yet the "voice" and the "vision" remain consistent. In other words, as Boyd says of Woolf, the writer "fragments the self, by giving it six voices that are different and yet the same" (106). Though Hinojosa does not produce novels that are "reflexive" to the extent that Boyd says Woolf does, he is in fact doing the same thing with his own voice, his own self. Hinojosa's own effort to forge for himself a balanced view of the Valley enables him to speak not only as Rafe, Jehú, and P. Galindo, but also through the voices of such reprobate characters as Noddy Perkins, Polín Tapia, Choche Markham, and others.

As Boyd says, "the book itself can create a condition in which it is possible for the writer to appear as someone [he] is not" and can serve as "an instrument for facilitating a 'natural' impersonation" (106). He further argues his point by saying that the proof that Woolf *is* in fact "A Voice in Search of Six Speakers" is found "when the writer compares the language of the created self to the 'real' self and finds that they match" (106). Hinojosa has said, "what you see here, this professor, and what ideas I may present, is what you will see in my writings: the voice doesn't vary" ("A Voice of One's Own" 14). Further, any reader who has heard Hinojosa speak or who has read any of his comments on his life and work must make the comparison Boyd speaks of. And such a reader must conclude that this "matching" solves the problem of point of view—it is really a consistent point of view filtered through the various voices of the "characters."

In *Seduction and Betrayal*, Elizabeth Hardwick says of *The Waves*, "the people are not characters," in the sense of, say, a Jane Austen character, and "there is not plot in usual sense" (136). In Woolf's novel, as well as in Hinojosa's work, this phenomenal absence of two of the necessary ingredients of "fiction"—plot and character—requires that something take their place to provide consistency and continuity. That *something*, in Hinojosa's case, is the voice of the author. Boyd's argument may seem obvious: all writers speak through their characters. But there is more going on here. Boyd claims that "the text of *The Waves* is not *about* the act of self-creation through language but rather it *is* such an act" (107 emphasis in original). This statement is particularly applicable to what Hinojosa is doing in the *Death Trip* sequence, and most obviously in the *Korean Love Songs*, *The Useless Servants*, *Rites and Witnesses*, *Dear Rafe*, and much of *Claros Varones de Belken*.

Hinojosa is making sense of his own past and quantifying his own identity; in fact, he forges his own identity by "documenting" and ordering his experience through his writing. The autobiographical nature of the *Klail City Death Trip Series* insists on this interpretation. Hinojosa says, "What I worked on, as far as my life was concerned, was toward a personal voice which was to become my public voice" ("A Voice of One's Own" 13). Jill Johnston argues that "when we write the life, we are making it up," so that "we can endlessly move [the facts] around, make them do things, act on them, pitch them in different contexts" (29). As there is in *The Waves*, there is in Hinojosa's work an "open acknowledgment of the presence of a self that is neither wholly fictional nor wholly real, but a 'presence,' attempting to catch itself in the act of self-creation" (Boyd 116). Though it belongs more to the early period than to this transitional period, P. Galindo's manifesto in *Klail City* is the best example of this presence. In those sections entitled *The Searchers* we have to wonder whether it is the migrant workers or P. Galindo (and Rolando Hinojosa) who is seeking something, attempting to "catch" something. Rolando Hinojosa creates and continually recreates himself as P. Galindo, Rafe Buenrostro, Jehú

Malacara, et. al. through the creation of the *Klail City Death Trip Series*. P. Galindo all but admits this, particularly in his insistence on calling himself "the wri" (*el esc* in the Spanish version). The voices of Rafe in *Korean Love Songs* and *The Useless Servants*, of Jehú in *Dear Rafe*, and of both in *Claros Varones de Belken* also reveal Hinojosa's personal efforts to come to terms with himself and to express that self.

Hinojosa again reveals the autobiographical nature of his works when he explains in a 1988 interview why he used Spanish and then English in *Claros Varones de Belken*: "The generation that I know very well, my generation, we were in our twenties then, so we still had one leg in the Spanish background, and an emerging leg in the English background" (Dasenbrock 3). Though P. Galindo can first be identified as Hinojosa in *Klail City*, this peculiarly autobiographical element of Hinojosa's fiction is most evident in the middle period, the period covering the years when Hinojosa had to decide who he was to be. He reveals his ambivalence when he says

> At times, I wonder about those who choose adaptation over true happiness in a desire to please others; and I wonder, but not for very long, about those who ignore, and about those who choose to deny the existence of at least two cultures and of the complex symbi-

otic relationship inherent in the various
Texas cultures. It must be a strange world,
this ostrich-like existence and attitude. ("AQ
Voice of One's Own" 14)

Despite this commentary, he himself has chosen an
"adaptation" in that he is neither living the life of the
characters depicted in the novels, nor living in the
Valley any longer, but he also has to face up to the
"symbiotic relationship" within his worlds, and it is
the nature and meaning of this relationship that
shapes the *Death Trip*. His characters as well must
learn to adapt as they grapple with the complexity of
their world. Hinojosa's "presence" or "self" is also felt
in the late works, as Becky Caldwell/Escobar/
Malacara is also revealed to be a version of Hinojosa.
By the time of *Becky*, Hinojosa has in essence "finished" Jehú and Rafe, so he salvages the not-very-
appealing Becky Escobar and turns her into a female
version of Jehú and Rafe. In *Becky and Her Friends*,
we see a young woman leaving an unsatisfying marriage (a good topical subject), but we also see a young
Mexican American learning to speak Spanish—re-
claiming a portion of her heritage, and another reflection of Hinojosa's ambivalence about "adaptation."
    Hinojosa's comment in *The Valley* that "what fol-
lows, more likely as not, is a figment of someone's
imagination" reveals not so much his confidence in

his creative imagination as his struggle to *find*—or create if necessary—a self-identity and his doubts (at first) about being able to do so. Is he creating himself? Are outside forces altering the self he is trying to create?

That Hinojosa is engaged in producing a sequence novel is not surprising, in light of his interest in history (a necessary component of his self-discovery), and also because as Boyd says, it is not possible to realize or grasp one's "self-creation," and so, "by its very impossibility," one is driven to a "continuance of the effort" (116). Boyd also acknowledges that using autobiographical materials opens up numerous possibilities:

> Joyce's extensive use of autobiographical materials points not so much to a failure of the imagination as to a blurring of the boundaries between fiction and non-fiction, between imagination and memory. A curious process of leveling sets in . . . whereby what *did* happen, what *could* happen, and what might *yet* happen all coalesce on a single fictional plane. (121, emphasis in original)

Boyd's comment about "leveling" echoes Hinojosa's (and his characters') repeated claims that time is the greatest leveler. So autobiography, according to Boyd,

is always tempered or smoothed out by time, a point
of view Hinojosa would seem to agree with. "Fact"
and imagination (created "facts") become one and the
same, or at least of the same value.

Of related interest is the "blurring of boundaries"
that Boyd speaks of. In discussing Faulkner's *Absalom, Absalom!* in a chapter subtitled, "Fiction as
History," Boyd says that "The life that the novel describes is the life that it creates, and that life is no
less *there* than the events that compose our histories. In fact, it is *all* there, in a way that even the
most complete historical study is not" (67, emphasis
in original). As R. W. B. Lewis has said of Hawthorne's
"Earth's Holocaust," "like every good story, it was
truer than history" (14). For Hinojosa, this recreated
world tells his whole story, his truth, in a way that
strict autobiography could not.

Steven Kellman, in *The Self-Begetting Novel*,
quotes Henry Miller on the subject:

> The autobiographical novel, which Emerson
> predicted would grow in importance with
> time, has replaced the great confessions. It
> is not a mixture of truth and fiction, this
> game of literature, but an expansion and
> deepening of truth. It is more authentic, more
> veridical, than the diary. It is not the flimsy
> truth of facts which the authors of the auto-

> biographical novels offer, but the truth of
> emotion, reflection and understanding, truth
> digested and assimilated. (117)

Hinojosa has referred to "truth, that necessary element" (*Dear Rafe* 7) in more than one place. And with
his insistence on the past in all its manifestations,
with Jehú and Rafe looking back at their own distant and more recent pasts, with their listening to
other voices recounting their boyhoods (as when
Echevarría tells of Rafe's father's death), Hinojosa is
striving to present "the truth of emotion, reflection
and understanding, truth digested and assimilated,"
rather than a strictly historical or autobiographical
account, because the former is capable of expressing
what could have happened, what *might* have happened, and possibly what *did* happen, or at least a
perception of what happened. But it is richer and
fuller than autobiography because it allows a deeper
exploration of Rolando Hinojosa (in the guise of many
characters) than does a report of what *actually* happened. Hinojosa can act out a variety of parts, to show
a complete picture of himself.

Hinojosa downplays the historical forces which
compel the assertion of his characters' identities. The
complexity of racial prejudice, war, familial and communal relationships figure throughout the series, but
ultimately it is the way a character *responds* to events,

not the events themselves, which shape character. Jill
Johnston says that by writing one's life, one engages
in "a political act of self-recognition," an act which
requires acknowledgement of shaping forces in one's
life, but which refuses to be subjugated by those forces
(29). Hinojosa's achievement lies somewhere between
these two experiences.

Kellman's argument for the uniqueness of American literature also helps to put the *Death Trip* in perspective. He claims that much of American literature
is about "the intentional creation of a home, a nation, and a self where nothing had existed before"
(107). The *Death Trip* is about the creation of a home
(metaphorically), a resting place, and a self, created
not out of "nothing," but out of an obscurity and in-
visibility that is caused paradoxically by an old, distinct identity that is both "beloved and reviled" (*Claros
Varones* 208). It is an identity of race *and* culture, an
identity that in some way must be shed. Like
Hinojosa, Rafe and Jehú must come to terms with
the Anglo world, and in doing so they must recreate
themselves, doing away with bits and pieces of their
heritage, an experience akin to rummaging through
the attic and deciding what to keep and what to include in the jumble sale. This is a peculiarly American process and is unlike that of older cultures in
which experience is layered over the centuries; the

American impulse is to strip experience away to begin anew.[2]

Kellman says that this American trait has created a "distinctive national self-consciousness," which is "not so much a pensive ego reflecting back on itself as an ardent desire to create a self. . . . Abandoning an obsolete identity in Europe, pilgrims of every persuasion have been acutely aware of the need to construct another life in the wilderness across the Atlantic" (107). By analogy, Jehú and Rafe, like Hinojosa, are acutely aware that the "old ways" are becoming obsolete and that they must construct another life in that "wilderness" which is the Anglo world. To fail to do so is to fade into obscurity, or rather to remain there, having no significant public persona. Kellman goes on to say that "the [American] folk myth posits the existence of a 'territory ahead' free of the hierarchies and conventions of Aunt Sally's civilization. There individual worth and effort determine success" (108). For the Mexican American, this pervasive folk myth is up-ended: there is no true place of freedom beyond the hierarchies and conventions; the hierarchies and conventions are the wilderness or the frontier. Hinojosa's recognition of this myth accounts for at least part of his ironic point of view. A social and psychic rather than physical wilderness awaits Jehú and Rafe. Though Hinojosa is an ethnic or so-called "marginal" writer, ostensibly removed from the mainstream of American fiction, he is in fact writing about one of the major issues of American history and life. Only the perspective is altered.

The Mexican-American community in the Valley undergoes many changes in the middle novels. What was once an isolated, exploited minority slowly begins to move into the mainstream of American life. It is the changing *mejicano* community that Hinojosa observes so tellingly in the *Klail City Death Trip Series*. A community on the fringe, kept down and exploited, does not have the same concerns as the dominant community. As a result, the exploited community does not experience a cultural or philosophic movement at the same time as the dominant community. Within the United States, regionalist cultures have lagged behind the more urban and homogenized mainstream culture. After World War II, however, even regional cultures were dragged into the Modern Age to a degree not experienced even after World War I, a war that did not touch America in the same way that it did Europe. And, according to Carl Allsup, World War I significantly restricted any attempt by the Mexican-American community to move into the "modern" world of democracy and economic equity because it "institutionalized Mexican immigration as a 'special' necessity for American agriculture" (6). This fact strengthened the stereotype of the "Mexicans" (and that included Mexican Americans) as outsiders who were essentially un-American.

But World War II changed the life of rural Mexican Americans in a significant way. As Allsup points out, because military deferments were in the hands of local boards, few Mexican Americans received them. Hundreds of thousands of Mexican Americans served, and many were heroes. Twenty-five percent of the soldiers at Bataan were Mexican-American. Seventeen Mexican Americans were awarded the Congressional Medal of Honor, the most awarded to any ethnic group (Allsup 16). For many of these soldiers, their war experience was their first introduction to the outside world. Allsup notes that "the economic, political, and social relationships of New Mexico and Texas did not have the same meaning or influence in a European or Pacific war zone" that they had had at home (16). People who had been told repeatedly that they were inferior to Anglos now had reassurance for themselves and proof for everyone else that they were not.

But circumstances at home did not change so readily, and the government and press together helped to sustain the old stereotypes. Nevertheless, the Mexican-American community had had its eyes opened and began to feel a sense of empowerment. One returning soldier said of his war experience, "We were now admired, respected, and approved by all those around us, including most of our commanding officers" and this respect began to be felt in the community at large (Allsup 16). Allsup argues that the contrast between the Mexican American's experience in World War II and the world that awaited him at home was the real catalyst for change:

> The contrast between these two experiences, environments, and realities would produce important and substantive change in the methods, or more significant, the attitudes by which Mexican Americans attempted to deal with their needs. . . . A Chicano fighting against oppression in Germany should not have to fight for his people in Texas. In facing the political, economic, and social inequities of American society, many individuals faced themselves and their own concept of what their country could be or wanted to be. (17)

In addition, of course, what opened up the Mexican-American community in the Valley was in part what opened up the rest of rural America: improved communications, better educational opportunities, including the GI Bill, increased use of the automobile and public transportation, and television. If the experience of World War II created a readiness for change and a belief in the possibility of change, then the historical reality of mid-twentieth-century American life created the certainty of it.

What Hinojosa shows in his post-war novels is a community that has no choice but to enter the fray, be it eagerly or unwillingly. The complexity of the twentieth century has penetrated even that isolated and unique Mexican-American culture of the Río Grande Valley, and the Mexican American must now deal head-on with issues that have existed for several generations, but which now impel him to position himself on the front line. That Hinojosa's characters in the later novels have to deal with "contradictions," as Rosara Sánchez says, is caused not by a new political stance on Hinojosa's part, but simply by his recognition of a historical reality (Sánchez 76).

Hinojosa deals with the issues that face the Mexican-American community as the Río Grande Valley becomes less heterogeneous and more fragmented, when young men no longer assume that they will be agricultural workers, but find their way to college (often with the help of the GI Bill) or infiltrate the conservative business establishments of the Anglo. Jehú and Rafe are typically "American" in their pursuit of a new life, a life dependent in large part on whether one makes it through the university, that bastion of Anglo culture. The significance of a university education is reiterated throughout the sequence, and some of Hinojosa's most visible characters after *The Valley* and *Klail City* are either university-educated (Rafe, Jehú, Becky) or have traveled extensively and lived outside the Valley, perhaps even in Europe (Viola Barragán). At the same time, Hinojosa shows the Mexican American's reluctance to entirely abandon his identity (if it were actually possible to do so). As Miguel Léon-Portillo notes,

> it is undeniable that cultural identity can persist despite multiple processes of change, including the assimilation of foreign elements and even the abandonment of other elements that had belonged to the group. . . . [I]t is also clear that certain alterations and losses may seriously harm an identity. (22)

In these works, Jehú maintains his identity in a variety of ways, but most particularly by keeping a hypercritical eye on the way the Anglo community operates and attempts to manipulate the "upwardly mobile" Mexican American. His response to the Anglos' complicated efforts at control is often humorous, but it is also always marked by an insight that reveals his essential distrust of Anglo motives. Jehú seems willing to tolerate a certain amount of manipulation, as long as he knows it is going on, which gives him a measure of control over it. His relationship with Noddy Perkins of the Klail City Bank is one example of this. And as he says in response to the Anglo woman who wonders how many Mexicans Noddy Perkins invited to his party, "I think it's healthy to hear this type of shit once in a while; it's both sobering and reassuring that all's not well with the world" (*Dear Rafe* 21). Clearly, the new world is as yet unborn.

Rafe's role in the works of this period becomes clear only through a reading of *The Useless Servants*. He is a ghost-like figure in the epistolary novel *Dear Rafe*, never answering the letters sent by Jehú—or at least we never see his replies. *Dear Rafe* seems more like a journal kept by Jehú than any means of real communication between two people, yet it merits attention because of its form: the letters Jehú writes to Rafe are among the few documents in the entire series that might be taken entirely as they appear, without wariness. We have to assume that what Jehú says to Rafe is as close to "truth" as any commentary in the series might be.

Most of *Dear Rafe* is concerned with the bank and the political and business world of the Anglos of Klail City, along with an occasional comment on Jehú's love life. There is some humor in Jehú's accounts of these things, but it is not the kind of humor found in *The Valley* or *Klail City*. There is nothing here, for instance, to compare to the Bruno Cano escapade in the cemetery, Aunt Chedes's attacks, or some of Brother Imas's sermons. The letters from Jehú to Rafe lack the multiple voices that create the dynamism of the earlier works, and even in the second part of the novel, the "reportage" section, the material is presented in a very tidy, orderly way, with very little shifting in chronology, very little digression, very little humor.

Though the first part of *Dear Rafe* is an epistolary novel, its most significant technical aspect is that it is "a work that is contained within a framing level of narration," what Margarita Cota-Cárdenas calls a *relato enmarcado* (159). She points out that *Don Quixote* is also such a work, but she might have mentioned any number of other works, including Hawthorne's *The Scarlet Letter* and John Fowles's *The French Lieutenant's Woman*. In *Dear Rafe*, Hinojosa uses his surrogate, P. Galindo, in a bold and dramatic way. His technique borders on metafiction, for the reader is well aware of how the "author," or "the writer" P. Galindo, got the story and how he created it. P. Galindo, dying of cancer in the William Barrett Veterans Hospital, somehow "receives" a packet of letters written in the fairly recent past by Jehú Malacara to his cousin Rafe Buenrostro, who was convalescing there after surgery on his face, which was pelted by shrapnel during his service in Korea. (That Rafe's face is physically "altered" is clearly symbolic of the larger and just as painful alternative that his inner "face" must undergo.) At the present time, Rafe is a non-practicing attorney and a lieutenant in the Belken County District Attorney's office.[3] Jehú's whereabouts are unknown. As P. Galindo says at the conclusion of the prologue, "As for Jehú, there's no telling where he is, and hence this story" (9).

Galindo's presence is felt in a number of other works in the sequence, for along with Rafe and Jehú, he is one of the principal narrators or surrogate authors, speaking in Hinojosa's own voice. Cota-Cárdenas has noted that the voices of P. Galindo and Jehú in *Dear Rafe* have in common "a restrained humor" (160). Juan Bruce-Novoa has commented on the similarity between the voice in the work and the voice of the author himself, saying that "Hinojosa the man is the reflection of his work: eloquent, intelligent . . . ironic, sometimes sharp and critical, but with the constant good humor of a man who knows human nature" ("Rolando" 51). In *Dear Rafe*, P. Galindo says that he feels "all bases" are not covered in Part I (the letters), so in Part II he "intends to add a shading of his own once in a while, but always on the side of truth, that necessary element" (*Dear Rafe* 7). In Part II, P. Galindo interviews his "informants" about the reasons for Jehú's flight from Klail City. The one thing that becomes clear from the dialogues and monologues in this part of the novel is that Jehú has an elusive personality like Rafe's. What follows is a "Penultimate Note" from P. Galindo on having to choose a stopping point (he has more material) and then a sort of summary entitled, "Brass Tacks are Best; They Last Longer," in which P. Galindo muses over the "evidence" presented in the first two parts of the novel. Here he affirms that though most of the *mejicanos* in Klail City believe Jehú left town under a cloud, they do not know what he is supposed to have done. Galindo then recounts the various versions of the "truth" that he has heard and concludes by saying that people usually have their way "when it comes to interesting stories that do not coincide with evident truth" (133).

Dear Rafe presents a clear picture of the ways in which the Texas Valley is slowly beginning to change. Jehú himself, as a sort of Everyman, is representative of that change. He feels the resistance to it, but he also perceives its inevitability. In addition, he is "lost"; he has not yet found a suitable or comfortable way to respond to these changing times. He is adrift, hard to pin down, just as Rafe is ephemeral and distant, just another number in a hospital ward, waiting. The circumstances Rafe and Jehú are in at the end of *Dear Rafe*—one confined, a sort of prisoner within an institution, and the other lost, both literally and figuratively—symbolize the trauma involved in assimilation and the difficulty of establishing a new identity. In fact, at this point, their situations reflect what Juan Bruce-Novoa has said of the Chicano, that they are "victims lost in and condemned by their geographical happenstance" ("Chicanos" 57). Yet Hinojosa does not allow his characters to remain lost or to be condemned by the accident of birth, and both these characters re-emerge as strong figures later in the series. But before that happens, they are both tested: Jehú is forced to be both a participant and an observer of small-town drama unfolding, as the haves and the have-nots come face to face on shifting ground, just as Rafe not only participates in but also observes the drama of war in *Korean Love Songs* and *The Useless Servants*.

To give an account of Rafe's Korean War service, Hinojosa relies on two books. The one in verse, *Korean Love Songs*, was—until the publication of *The Useless Servants* in 1993—the pivotal volume in his series. The poems of *Korean Love Songs* are similar to the dialogues and monologues of the novels, while *The Useless Servants* is a more detailed account in the form of a diary and is far superior as a work of art. Unfortunately, Arte Publíco Press omitted six crucial pages from *The Useless Servants* when it was published in hardback. Jaime Armin Mejía published the missing pages and an explanation of them in *Southwestern American Literature* ("Breaking" 1–6). These "found" pages function almost as a kind of

epiphany for Rafe as he recognizes fully the true nature of war and its impact upon human beings. These
pages, directed to the psychiatrist Dr. Perlman, are a
torrent of emotion that flows directly from Rafe's experience and his recognition of the fact that he and
most of his fellow soldiers are nothing more than children, trapped in the dark and nightmarish world that
Matthew Arnold so eloquently describes in "Stanzas
from the Grand Chartreuse"—"Wandering between
two worlds, one dead/The other powerless to be born."

   When he was first trying to decide how to deal
with Rafe's experience in the Korean War, Hinojosa
read the British poets who wrote about World War I.
He says that he eventually "got the idea that maybe
[he] should use poetry to render something as brutal
as war" (José David Saldívar, "Our Southwest" 181).
And according to Donald Randolph, Hinojosa wrote
to him in 1984 that "Careful rereading . . . of Blunden,
Brooke, Isaac Rosenberg, Graves' Goodbye and Sas-
soon's prose and poetry (and some Jarrell and
Shapiro) were of inestimable assistance. The Bible,
of course, is never far away, as are not, too, the clas-
sics" ("Eroticism" 219). Nevertheless, Hinojosa is primarily a fiction writer, not a poet. The result of his
effort is less poetry than it is a series of vignettes,
but overall the book is an effective metaphor for the
entire *Death Trip* sequence: just as Rafe will never
be the same after his war experience, the world of

the Río Grande Valley in the second half of the twentieth century can never be like the world that existed
until then. There is now a turn in the road.

With the 1993 publication of *The Useless Servants*, Hinojosa both complicates and clarifies the
character of Rafe Buenrostro and, by extension, the
Death Trip Series as a whole. It is in *The Useless Servants* that Rafe becomes a fully developed character
in a way not allowed to him in *Korean Love Songs*,
thus illuminating and expanding his role in the other
novels and creating a new perspective from which to
view the series itself. Not only do we see Rafe revealed
in a much more intimate way than in any of the earlier novels, but also, as Mejía asserts, the battle scenes
provide "experiences forming a fuller character development for Rafe" ("Breaking the Silence" 96).[4] We
also see Rafe's Korean War experience with complete
lucidity for the first time; as a result, it is finally possible to assess the full effect of such a catastrophic
experience as war on the individual character and
its reverberations on the Mexican-American community itself. Even more than the "vignettes" found in
the poems of the earlier *Korean Love Songs*, the detailed accounts of war in Rafe's diary bring his experience into relief when viewed against the backdrop
of his life at home, his life in the Valley—the life depicted so vividly in *The Valley*, *Klail City*, and parts of
Claros Varones de Belken.

Though only marginally "literary"—(with references to Rafe's reading, college, Catholic school)—*The Useless Servants* does reveal the young Rafe to be a literary type who clearly has some ambition to write and some talent for it. Interestingly, it is Hinojosa who turns out to be the writer. It is also interesting to see a picture of a young Rolando Hinojosa in his service uniform on the book jacket. The last we see of Rafe, he is a homicide detective in Belken County rather than a writer. Nevertheless, it is Rafe's acute observations and sensitive descriptions of events that bring *The Useless Servants* to life. The triteness of the phrase "all the usual horrors of war" is displaced by a definite sense of reality. Hinojosa, through Rafe's journal, brings us face to face with war. Though Rafe writes of the folks back home as having "no idea what goes on out there, what happens to us, what we see and do," *The Useless Servants* supplies the gruesome facts (167).

It is all there: the physical discomfort, the bad food, the uncertainty, the fear, the confusion, and the chaos, the boredom and the routine, the blood, the stench, and death. And of course the irony, which for Hinojosa's characters always serves as a release valve. Yet in *Servants*, the irony is often secondary to, or even absent from, Rafe's account of his wartime life. Some horrors, it seems, cannot be shrugged off, and sometimes Rafe cannot hide behind an ironic facade.

In his distress over the slaughter of refugees who are trying to cross a bridge that had been ordered destroyed, for instance, Rafe recounts the event dispassionately at first:

> And then, the bridge was destroyed. Blown up. Hundreds on it: kids, families, animals. Joey and I turned our backs to avoid seeing the bodies. The bridge was blown up in all kinds of pieces. A roar, a geyser of water and who knows what else went up in the air. All the time, our vehicles revving the motors, but we could still hear the screaming and crying. (35)

Later Rafe and his fellow soldiers try to explain to themselves why such a thing could happen; an officer tells them that it's too bad they had to see civilians killed, but he promises them that they will see worse. This incident recurs in Rafe's memory again and again, and his last comment on the day the bridge is destroyed is "For all the talk, there's nothing the army can do about what one thinks, and one does think, and remember" (37). Other atrocities occur: U.S. soldiers are captured and tortured before being executed; British soldiers are killed by friendly fire as the U.S. Air Force is confused about targets and geography; a "massacre" occurs that reminds one sol-

dier of all the pictures he's seen of Gettysburg; a fa-
vorite officer commits suicide. Yet the explosion of the
bridge is Rafe's true initiation into the senselessness
of war.

Despite Rafe's acknowledgement of the horror
and futility of war, he remains strong. His sense of
himself and his pride in his performance are evident
throughout the book, and early on he writes that he
knows why he couldn't turn and run from a battle, no
matter how frightened he might be. It is in Rafe's
sense of himself, his rootedness, that Hinojosa's regionalism surfaces in *Servants*:

> I know why I didn't run. Joey, Charlie, and I
> were all born in Klail City, TX. We enlisted
> together, and how would it look if I ran? Ev-
> erybody back home would know of it. I'd die
> first before I'd face that. (27)

These lines reveal Rafe's valid fear of being killed in
battle, along with his youthful fear of being ridiculed,
and somewhere in between the two lies his sense of
duty and obligation, not just to himself, but to his
fellow soldiers, his country, and more specifically to
the folks "back home," an obligation to represent them
well. Later when he is in the hospital in Tokyo, he
tries to explain himself to the psychiatrist Dr.
Perlman:

> I explained that we were different; that that part of Texas is *home, our* home. We're not like the rest of the guys in the United States, and many of them talk about moving to California, wherever. We *can't*, and we don't want to either. That some of us leave for a while, but that we have to come back. Home. And so on. (167)

In this entry he reflects on a world that is disintegrating, but Rafe doesn't realize that just yet. He doesn't realize just how much or in what ways this war will change him either. Hinojosa's title, *The Useless Servants*, taken from Luke 17:10, suggests that Rafe must do more than is normally required: "Well, will we then be like the useless servants who did nothing more than that which was commanded of us?" (184). Rafe, it seems, did more, winning two Purple Hearts (the first of which he sees ironically as "payment" for a wound—the second he "earned") and a Bronze Star. Yet his most significant action may have been the writing he did, his effort to immortalize those with whom he fought and to delineate the human face of battle. That some of the journals are "lost" is immaterial, for that does not mean that they are destroyed or that they will never be read by anyone.

The regional motif, along with its primary subtext, the race issue, surfaces from time to time, in

the character of Captain Bracken, the Texas Anglo
who is, as Joey says, "To the manner born" (152); in
Rafe's comment that if someone had "ever gone
through rank racial discrimination in Texas, then he
could talk to me about brotherhood" (151); in the character of Donald Trujillo, who won't speak Spanish.
Charlie and Joey scoff at Trujillo's statement that his
people came from Spain. They ask him "if those were
the Spaniards that landed in Virginia and then
trekked across the South until delivered safely and
soundly to the Promised Land" (41). Yet these incidents and comments, along with Rafe's sense of place
and history, cannot dispel the fact that Rafe sees everyone—including the enemy and civilians—as being in it together. He finally comes to terms even with
Bracken and says, "Captain Bracken showed up again
two days ago. We talked, and I felt I've no resent-
ments about anything, and I doubt I'll ever be angry
at anyone anymore" (168). In an echo of lines from
other novels in the series, Frazier says to Rafe, "No
battle lasts a hundred years" (126).

Rafe's comments are not surprising, given the
kinds of experience he has endured. Anger and re-
sentment seem out of place in the face of war. Rafe
reveals his emotions in entry after entry. In some
ways, *The Useless Servants* serves as a vehicle by
which Hinojosa can develop Rafe's character in much
the same way that *Dear Rafe* gives us our best glimpse

of Jehú Malacara. In the Chapter "Hoengsong," Rafe
writes,

> On the first day of the death count, I got off
> the two-and-a-half ton truck at the assem-
> bly point and threw up. Tried a cigarette and
> got the dry heaves immediately afterward
> .... Done in, I climbed in the back of a cov-
> ered weapons carrier, had a good cry, and that
> brought some peace. (135)

Later in the same chapter, he writes, "I'll never get
used to any of this," (135) and "I'm scared to talk to
the guys about Hoengsong; I'm trying to forget the
dead, but it isn't working out. Please, God, don't let
me go crazy" (139).

In addition to the obvious usefulness of these
entries—insight into Rafe's character, vivid description of the battlefield, etc.—is the insight we gain from
his double-edged cry of "I'm trying to forget the dead,"
for Rafe in later years must forget, or at least put
aside, these dead, just as he ultimately must put aside
a dead past. As he moves from the middle of the twentieth century toward the end of it, he must come to
terms with loss of all sorts. On the killing fields of
Korea he begins learning how to deal with such loss.

Though less intensely personal than *The Useless
Servants*, *Korean Love Songs* operates as well from a

broad and a narrow perspective. Because it is set outside the actual community of the Valley, Hinojosa is able to speak to issues of war without getting bogged down in the Mexican/Anglo question, although there is no doubt that he is aware of the hypocrisy inherent in a system that asks "second-class citizens" to give their lives for their country. Hinojosa's criticism of the system, however, is aimed at both the inherent horrors of war and issues of race and class, and of course is partly shaped by his awareness of his ethnicity and how it has affected his life thus far.

Korean Love Songs, like *The Useless Servants*, takes into account Rafe's awareness of racial slurs and racial ignorance, as in the poem entitled, "The Eighth Army at the Chongchon." General Walton H. (Johnny) Walker tells the troops, "We should not assume that (the) / Chinese Communists are committed in force. / After all, a lot of Mexicans live in Texas" (11). He also deals with the issue of race and ethnicity in "Nagoya Station," "Brief Encounter," and "Up Before the Board." These poems are about Sonny Ruiz, who fills in his own missing-in-action papers and then walks away to a new life in Japan. "Not long after, cards started to arrive from Nagoya and signed / By Mr. Kazuo Fusaro who, in another life, / Had lived as David Ruiz in Klail City" (43). When Rafe asks him about home, he answers, "*This* is home, Rafe. Why should I go back?" Rafe realizes he cannot answer:

"He has me there. Why, indeed?" (44). Ramón Saldívar argues that for Rafe to assert himself as an individual he must "regain that preseparatist expression which has been the legacy of his people" (*Chicano Narrative* 145). If by this, Saldívar means that in order to forge an identity Rafe must go backward in time and back to a culture which, though once intact, is no longer, then Rafe has an impossible journey before him, for none of us, no matter what our past or our history, can regress in such a way. Though Rafe may attempt just such a journey, though he may desire such a destination, even were it possible, he would not find at his journey's end that "preseparatist collective expression" which, like the idea of a Deerslayer, is a dream, an ideal.

    Here again, Rafe is not really aware of the sort of loss that is coming or the magnitude of the changes that are occurring; Sonny perhaps sees the past as already dead, or perhaps chooses to defect rather than face battles back home after the war is over. Rafe, however, and others like him, will face those battles which will be in many ways as harsh as the ones found in wartime. As Ramón Saldívar notes, "Rafe chooses not to turn against his American home" (*Chicano Narrative* 146). Sonny pulls off his defection because Rafe, considered by the Board of Inquiry to be "a good man" helps him:

You see, I'm what's considered to be
"A good man." In their view,
One who won't cry, carp, complain, cower, or
      crap in his pants.
A good man. Yessir. One of the best.
And so, I lie. (49)

Rafe's response is existentialist, as is his "explanation" of why he is lying after swearing to tell the truth
on "a Government Issued bible":

If you're a well-fed monk
Who's tired of womanizing, and who's hap-
      pened to hit on the idea that
No man is an island,
well and good.
But Tina Ruiz [Sonny's mother] needs some-
      thing to eat and to live on. (49)

Rafe lies not only for Sonny's sake, but also for Sonny's
widowed mother back home in Klail City. Rafe's ironic
reference to Donne shows that he does not see Sonny's
defection or "death" as diminishing himself in the
least, which is in direct contrast to his own explanation as to why *he* could not "run." It's a practical rather
than a philosophical matter here, whereas in *The
Useless Servants* it is clearly the opposite.

Even though Hinojosa treats the issue of race from time to time, it is difficult to read *Korean Love Songs* as a border ballad, a *corrido*, as Rámon Saldívar does in a Marxist interpretation of the book (R. Saldívar, "Korean," 143). More accurate is the fact that Rafe and all the other soldiers are pawns of the vast military machine. As Serge Ricard has noted, Hinojosa makes this clear when "Boston John" wonders "what he is doing hee-ah" ("Rolando Hinojosa" 155). The war machine cares little for them as individuals no matter what their race, although Rafe's situation is touched by a higher irony: he is a second-class citizen at home. Saldívar does, however, perceive the work as a metaphor for change: He says that it "is about South Texas and Mexican-American life in a moment of crucial self-definition" ("Korean" 147). Saldívar is right in that *Korean Love Songs*—and *The Useless Servants*—signal a change in the life of the individual character, Rafe Buenrostro, and in the historical facts that shaped the life of the Mexican-American community during that period following World War II when ideas of Mexican-American liberation began to grow. It signals a change in *time*, a concept of great interest to Hinojosa throughout the *Death Trip* sequence.

Korean Love Songs and *The Useless Servants* are something of an anomaly in the body of Hinojosa's

work; they differ markedly from the other books because they are set outside the Valley and lack the
numerous voices of most of the other works. As a result, the presence of the community is not felt, really
for the first time. Even after Hinojosa returns to the
Valley and uses voices from the community again,
the force of the community seems fragmented. *Korean Love Songs* and *The Useless Servants* signal a
change, a different outlook, in the *Death Trip Series*,
a more insistent focus on the individual rather than
on the whole community. The major characters rise
out of and above the community as the sequence
progresses. What Ramón Saldívar says of the *Death
Trip Series* as a whole, that the "novels create less a
history of individual subjects and unique personalities than a history of the collective social life" (*Chicano
Narratives* 141) is more accurate of *The Valley* and
Klail City than it is of *Dear Rafe*, *Rites and Witnesses*,
Korean Love Songs, or *The Useless Servants*.

P. Galindo, in *Klail City*, describes his efforts as
being "the reconstruction of an old house that needs
saving, holding on to; one begins with a bit of work
here and there, a bit of retouching, and all done care-
fully, lovingly, almost" (55). These lines very neatly
describe Hinojosa's method of reconstructing the
world of the Río Grande Valley in the pre-World War
II years, but they do not seem as clearly applicable to
the later works, especially those of the final period,

Partners and *Becky*. It is possible to argue that historical change in large measure dictates this change
in tone, which precipitates a loss of dramatic energy.

This change in tone is evident even in *Rites and
Witnesses*, the other novel of this period, which more
closely follows the format of the earlier works. *Rites*
is the most technically interesting of these three
works, with Hinojosa relying on shifting scenes, chronology, points of view. He shifts from a Molly Bloom-
like monologue delivered by Sammie Jo Perkins to a
scene from the war in Korea in which one of Rafe's
buddies goes hysterical (much like scenes from Ford
Madox Ford's *Parade's End* in which Christopher
Tietjens can't remember names), or from a dialogue
between Jehú and Noddy Perkins to an unidentified
narrator's commentary, or to an interior monologue
by Polín Tapia, all without any transition. These techniques are familiar mainstays of the earlier works,
and Hinojosa uses them more or less successfully
here, but they somehow fail to create worlds of full-
ness and vitality like those found in *The Valley* and
Klail City, perhaps because those earlier worlds no
longer exist.

Claros Varones de Belken, written about 1979–
80 but not published until 1986, contains Rafe's recounting of his and Jehú's time together at the University of Texas—some three years after they returned
from Korea. Rafe recounts some of the experiences

he had returning to civilian life, doing odd jobs before going off to the university, and then Jehú tells of
their time spent teaching at Klail City High School
and their twentieth class reunion. (Some of this appears earlier in *Klail City*.) P. Galindo recounts a few
stories, the most notable being the affair of Rita Loera
and Moisés Guevara, and her husband Ignacio's hu-
miliation of both of them. In addition, P. Galindo an-
nounces that Esteban Echevarría (about eighty-
seven) has decided to die. (It is about 1959–60.) And
finally, Echevarría himself speaks, summing up the
history of the old community, or to use Arnold's term,
that "dead world": he says that the old life is "dead
and gone, dead and forgotten" (206). He concedes that
it is not entirely the fault of the Anglo: "There were
wholesale sellouts among our people" (206), but whatever the reasons, he tells Rafe, "you're a young man
who lives among the old and who lives with their old
memories" (208). And yet, Echevarría is proud that
"the Valley's coming along" now, that so many of the
young people are becoming "u-ni-ver-si-ty gra-du-
ates," which "has a ring to it" (218). So even though
Echeverría's day is over, he anticipates the dawn of a
new one. That new day is the problem Hinojosa tries
to deal with in the final two (chronological) novels of
the series.

  The works of the middle period—*Korean Love
Songs*, *The Useless Servants*, *Claros Varones de Bel-*

ken, *Rites and Witnesses*, and *Dear Rafe*—piece together a bridge between the old and the new. A world
only hinted at in the earlier works of *The Valley* and
Klail City becomes the focus of these later works. This
is a world of change and yet it is far removed from
the world of *Partners in Crime* and *Becky and Her
Friends*, where it would seem that racial discrimination has all but disappeared, young Mexican-American women may challenge traditional female roles,
and university degrees are the order of the day. In
the world of *Rites and Witnesses*, change is slow to
come to the Valley, and resistance is on every side.
The Anglo resistance is not surprising, but the Mexican American has to learn to adapt to change also.
The trauma of change is felt both communally and
individually, as relations between the two communities become more varied. Stock answers no longer
suffice, and new ways of dealing with one another
must be found.

---

[1] Erlinda Gonzáles-Berry discusses this aspect of Hinojosa's
fiction in *"Estampas del Valle*: From Costumbrismo to Self-Reflecting Literature."

[2] See Mark Busby, "The Significance of the Frontier in Contemporary American Fiction." This is an enlightening essay on
the power of frontier mythology in twentieth-century American
literature.

[3] The chronology is confused, partly because when Hinojosa translated *Mi querido Rafa* as *Dear Rafe*, he made Rafe a non-practicing attorney and police detective in Belken County. He mentions this in the opening of *Dear Rafe* and in a couple of Jehú's letters to him. None of this is mentioned in *Mi querido Rafa*. Possibly Hinojosa made these changes because *Partners in Crime*, like *Dear Rafe*, was published in 1985, and he wished to establish a new persona for the crime novel.

[4] J. A. Mejía, in "Breaking the Silence" comments that Hinojosa's separate language renditions of the same narrative are different, as one language edition will include narrative information not found in the other language edition. Thus, Mejía believes, both language editions have to be read in order to obtain a comprehensive contextual and intertextual interpretation of what are ultimately the same serial narratives. Many critics and reviewers of Hinojosa's serial texts, says Mejía, have committed serious interpretative errors because they failed to read different renditions of the same serial narrative.

This charge is both pedantic and unfounded, if only for the reason that Hinojosa himself has chosen to *recreate* his early Spanish-language works in English since at least 1978, and has written his most recent novels in English. That simple fact proves that he has made an effort to produce a coherent body of work in English, largely because he realizes that his potential audience is for the most part English-speaking. It would surely prove to be an interesting study—in the way that, say, a study of all the drafts of Ulysse*s* would be interesting—to see a complete textual comparison of those works that were written in both English and Spanish, but to argue that this is the *only* way to appreciate the *Death Trip Series* is to belittle Hinojosa's efforts.

6

The End of a Journey

Partners in Crime and *Becky and Her Friends* mark a significant change in the *Klail City Death Trip* sequence. Ostensibly, these two works are meant to continue Hinojosa's exploration of his major subject: the evolving world of the Texas Valley as two cultures seek a new coexistence, and more particularly, the quest of Rafe Buenrostro and Jehú Malacara to create new identities for themselves, to establish themselves within the Anglo community. In these two novels, curiously, Hinojosa manipulates yet another permutation of the American myth. As Nicholas Karolides has noted, one manifestation (and there are many other contradictory and overlapping ones) of the American frontier mythol-

ogy is "the conflict between the wilderness ideal and
the cult of progress as represented by the culture of
civilized society" (11). One form that this conflict takes
is "the frontiersman against the settler," and "a free,
wandering life versus marriage, responsibility, set-
tling down" (11). In a sense, despite Rafe's success
within the Anglo establishment, he does live "a free,
wandering life" and his work—his daily life—deals
with a world of violence and crime that lies outside
the "culture of civilized society." Jehú, the alter ego,
works for the Klail City Bank, marries, and takes on
the upbringing of Becky's two children. In short, he
"settles down."

Whether the divergent paths taken by these two
characters is yet another expression of what Hinojosa
calls his "dual vision" or merely a convenience of plot
is not clear. What is clear is that the *Klail City Death
Trip Series* is shaped in a variety of ways by the pervasiveness of American myth. Nevertheless, the sequence breaks down in these two novels, in large part
because of Hinojosa's decision to include a work of
detective fiction, *Partners in Crime*, which seems
rather cavalierly inserted into a novel sequence that
has been moving forward in a more or less dramatically coherent way. In *Partners in Crime*, Hinojosa
leaves behind many of his familiar themes and characters to branch out into another fictional genre—
that of the police detective and his trials within the

strange and violent criminal subculture. New characters, new subject, new themes: an admirable attempt on the part of an author seeking to test his creative abilities, but by linking this novel to a fictional world whose parameters have already been clearly established, Hinojosa explodes those parameters and leaves the reader somewhat confused about the author's aims. With *Partners*, he fails to achieve continuity of any sort.[1] Though he is not producing the kind of sequence that depends on an absolutely strict chronology, in *Partners* he cuts nearly irrevocably the tenuous thread of continuity that holds the individual novels together. Only the presence of Jehú and Rafe sustains it.

Despite the many differences between the early novels of the *Klail City Death Trip Series* and *Partners in Crime*, Hinojosa attempts to establish a link between them, primarily in the characters of Rafe Buenrostro, who is the central figure in *Partners*, and Jehú Malacara, who plays an important though small part in the plot. These two figures have functioned as the major characters—although often offstage—in all of the previous novels. And yet they do not belong to this world of detective fiction: they seem out of place, lacking the community that has supported them, at least partially, in all of the earlier works, and which Hinojosa attempts to retrieve in *Becky*. Jehú is more himself, more recognizable, than is Rafe, who seems to have become another character entirely, except perhaps for a few flashbacks of memory to the war in Korea, his conversations with Jehú and his sexual interludes with Sammie Jo Perkins, with whom he has had a long-running affair.

The focus of the *Klail City Death Trip Series* shifts altogether in *Partners* in spite of the presence of Rafe and Jehú. Hinojosa simply gives up the quest motif, suggesting that a resolution has been achieved. And apparently—from the author's point of view—it has, and not only for these particular characters, because Rafe and Jehú's progress, though mirroring Hinojosa's, has also served as a kind of Everyman's journey for the whole community. In *Partners*, Hinojosa suggests that the community has achieved resolution, but in doing so he loses control of the sequence.

In addition, Hinojosa almost entirely abandons the issues that inform the rest of the sequence: the problems of the ethnic community, the past; the eccentricities of various lives give way to a "modern society" where crime flourishes and violence is barely contained. And yet life looks pretty rosy overall in *Partners*. The novel offers no real resolution to the doubt and cynicism that trouble Rafe and Jehú in works such as *Korean Love Songs*, *The Useless Servants*, *Claros Varones de Belken*, *Rites and Witnesses*, and *Dear Rafe*. Like the historical change that provides the impetus for change in these transitional

novels, in *Partners* and *Becky*, Hinojosa proposes that
the civil rights movement has created real equality
and that Jehú's, Rafe's, and Becky's educations have
solved most of their problems, including questions of
self-identity. Hinojosa has said that in *Partners in
Crime* he is "coming up more and more to, say, 1972"
(Dasenbrock 4), but both *Becky* and *Partners* have a
decidedly eighties flavor to them.

There is no real evidence anywhere that these
characters should be so settled, so happy. When we
last saw Jehú and Rafe, they seemed afloat, troubled.
Though Rafe is little more than a shadow in *Dear
Rafe*, we do discover there that he is still bothered by
the injury he received in the Korean War and he is
still somehow isolated, a loner. His confinement in
the William Barrett Veterans Hospital is a metaphor
for his state of mind, an outlook shaped not only by
the Mexican-American condition, but also by his experiences of war. Jehú at the end of *Dear Rafe* is lost,
literally, in that no one in the community knows where
he has gone, and he offers no explanation. The gloom
of *Korean Love Songs* and *The Useless Servants*,
Echevarría's lament for the old, almost-forgotten stories, the wry and acute observations of *Rites and Witnesses*, and the sinister aspects of *Dear Rafe* are
glossed over by the upbeat and cheerful mood of both
Partners in Crime and *Becky and Her Friends*.

Chronologically the last novel of the sequence, *Becky and Her Friends* also suggests that all is well in the Valley now. As in *Partners*, self-determination is a fully attainable goal.[2] Most of Hinojosa's characters—and certainly the main characters—no longer have to worry about the conditions of migrant life or overt racism. The admirable characters now could be any American anywhere who has "made it." In fact, there is rarely even a small hint that some of the old problems of the community might still exist today, apparently because Hinojosa's characters now are a part of the Anglo community, much more so than they were just a few years before.[3] Ed García says that Hinojosa's "strongest criticism" and "broadest ridicule" are aimed at "those Mexicans who long for Anglo success," but García fails to see that although Hinojosa criticizes the likes of Uncle Tom-ish Polin Tapia and the toadying Ira Escobar—and all who allow themselves to be manipulated by the controlling powers of Belken County—he has only praise for the upwardly mobile superior types like Rafe, Jehú, Becky, and Viola Barragán. If these characters harbor a desire to beat the Anglo at his own game, the ultimate outcome of their victory is that they take one giant step into Anglo territory. Hinojosa has abandoned *la raza* to a large extent, focusing instead on a few "superior" individuals who have moved into the Anglo middle class. What Hinojosa attempts in *Part-*

ners in Crime and *Becky* brings to mind the comments of Alexis de Tocqueville:

> As social conditions become more equal, the number of persons increases who, although they are neither rich nor powerful enough to exercise any great influence over their fellows, have nevertheless acquired or retained sufficient education and fortune to satisfy their own wants. They owe nothing to any man; they acquire the habit of always considering themselves as standing alone, and they are apt to imagine that their whole destiny is in their own hands.
>
> Thus not only does democracy make every man forget his ancestors, but it hides his descendants and separates his contemporaries from him; it throws him back forever upon himself alone and threatens in the end to confine him entirely within the solitude of his own heart. (105–106)

The phrase "it throws him back forever upon himself alone" is an apt description of what happens to Rafe and Jehú as they experience the process of assimilation, yet Hinojosa all but ignores the depths of this traumatic experience, this death trip. What he promises in *Dear Rafe* is never fully delivered. Somewhere

between *Dear Rafe* and *Becky*, there is a missing novel.
Until that novel is written, the series will not be complete. This particularly difficult facet of the acculturation process—its isolation—cannot be denied. Just as
the westering frontiersman removed himself from a
world that was at least familiar to undergo his great
adventure, so must the Mexican American who participates fully in "American" society relinquish much
of his familiar ethnic culture. What Hinojosa fails to
document thoroughly is the deep psychological
trauma that must attend this process.

In addition, there is little to no integration of the
haves and have-nots among the Mexican Americans
in these two works. Brother Imás, Bruno Cano, and
others—even Echevarría who is remembered fondly
and respectfully—belong to another world. They do
not fit into the world of *Partners* and *Becky*, even
though some lip service is paid to the evils of social
climbing (Becky's forays into the women's clubs of
Klail, the "club wife" of a police officer, etc.).

The Mexican community is now fragmented, di-
vided in a way that it was not in *The Valley* and *Klail
City*. Though Hinojosa even in the early works plays
fair with the Anglo, still the conditions of life for most
Mexican Americans are painfully clear. Is Hinojosa
now suggesting that all is really and truly well for
the Mexican Americans in Belken County? If so, he
is deliberately laying aside the thing that gives the

early fiction its power—the full picture of a way of life. There is a blandness to the concerns and the world of these two novels; the atmosphere suggests the yuppie culture that pervaded the eighties, an ambience seen in other contemporary writers and in many popular movies. *Partners* and *Becky* are often grimly sincere. As Hinojosa's characters come forward in time, they become more earnest, with that kind of earnestness required of the upwardly mobile as they move from one social class to another. In many ways the fun goes out of them. It is as though Huck has decided to marry Becky Thatcher and bring up respectable children.

Hinojosa does attempt to reclaim his old subjects, his old characters, and his old community in *Becky and Her Friends*, but he has difficulty re-establishing the sense of community and sense of continuity that characterize the early novels, in part because of the intrusion of *Partners in Crime* into the series, but primarily because of the change in tone. Since the sequence ostensibly is to be a picture of the world of Belken County, Texas, from about 1920 to the present, one expects the community to play as vital a role in the later novels as it does in the earlier ones. But it does not. And the reason it does not is that as it turns out, the sequence ultimately is about the author and his negotiation of the complex world of the Anglo more than it is about the community as a whole. The intense focus on Rafe and Jehú in the second chronological period (*Korean Love Songs*, *The Useless Servants*, *Claros Varones*, *Rites and Witnesses*, and *Dear Rafe*) confirms the autobiographical nature of the series, and finally in *Partners* and *Becky*, with the author's own place in the Anglo world assured, it becomes difficult for Hinojosa to depict further struggles in his main characters. He himself has left the Valley and the old community, and no matter how keenly he may feel that loss, he cannot truly return. As Thomas Wolfe warned, "You can't go home again." Hinojosa has become "established," along with Rafe and Jehú, within the American middle class.

Hinojosa treats the character of Becky as he does that of Jehú and Rafe. Becky, like Jehú, "the uncommon banker" (*Partners in Crime* 155), and Rafe, the lawyer turned policeman, has many talents, though they remain hidden until she throws off her life with Ira Escobar. Becky has apparently never felt much overt discrimination. Yet she has suffered sexual discrimination: under her mother's thumb, she has married the obtuse Ira. The implication is that she could have chosen quite well for herself, had she been allowed to, and she does when she chooses Jehú. So the potential is there, and it is revealed by her relationship with Jehú and her business relationship with Viola Barragán, the business paragon, the practical, sensible, unsentimental female.[4]

Hinojosa likes so-called "masculine" qualities in women—Becky doesn't cry or get emotional about her divorce, has a "good head for business," is unsentimental about sex and apparently everything else. All this makes getting what you want easy, as it apparently is for Viola and Becky. And if they don't get what they want immediately, they'll simply make a plan. Life is simple. Becky, like Jehú, Rafe, and P. Galindo before her, is a surrogate for the author. She too is on a quest. She is struggling to throw off an old identity, an old stereotype (the submissive Mexican wife and daughter), and she is struggling (and succeeds in the space of one book) to make it in the Anglo world. Like Hinojosa, Becky has an Anglo parent, Catarino Caldwell, who has "mexicanized" himself. Still, the Anglo influence is there. Like Hinojosa, Becky does not look "Mexican." She is tall and has green eyes. And she grows up with an Anglo name. Much is made of her looks, as early as *Dear Rafe*, when Jehú speaks of her in his letters. Hinojosa's gender bias is evidenced by his emphasis on female characters' appearances, an emphasis not apparent in his descriptions of male characters. In at least this one detail Hinojosa's clumsiness at trying to deal with feminist issues is evident.

The feminist stance articulated by Becky provides Hinojosa with an opportunity to pick up his old subject of the shedding of one tradition in favor of another. He has already achieved resolution with his male characters, and in doing so he has lost his subject. He tries to return to it with *Becky*. Just as Jehú and Rafe had to shed much of their traditionally ethnic personas to develop a new way of living in the world, Becky has to shed much of the traditionally feminine in order to forge a new identity. Unfortunately, the feminist rhetoric prevalent throughout the novel weakens Hinojosa's efforts and makes the book sound like a tract of some sort, at least in those sections that actually concern themselves with Becky's new self. Ironically, once Hinojosa's characters, particularly Jehú, Rafe, and Becky, gain a new identity within the Anglo community structure, they lose their distinct outlines—they become generic, losing personality and definition.

A conspicuous absence of conflict between the two Valley cultures is evident in both *Partners* and *Becky*. Rafe and his Anglo colleagues are the very picture of "cop buddies" and their relationship is characterized by genial male humor, not racial tension.[5] Another way in which we know that the race situation is "corrected" is that in *Partners*, Sam Dorson, a member of the Homicide Squad, goes to the Klail City Bank for a car loan: the person who must approve his application is a *mejicano*: Jehú Malacara. Likewise, Becky is judged by Anglo and *mejicano* alike because of her "modern" ways and her decision to divorce Ira Escobar to marry Jehú, with whom she had an earlier affair. She is not troubled by race relations any more than Jehú now is, even though that issue was of definite importance in the six works of the previous period.

In addition to a loss of focus, these two novels are marred by a moralism that is not characteristic of the other works in the sequence. This moralism is less troubling in *Partners in Crime* because it is a typical feature of the mystery novel. But in *Becky and Her Friends* it becomes oppressive. *Becky* lacks any real dramatic development, and in the interviews that are actually about Becky the message is essentially repetitive—one is either for or against Becky and the "liberation" of the Mexican-American woman (at least young, college-educated, pretty ones like Becky and/ or gutsy, aggressive, handsome ones like Viola Barragán).

Becky seems like an afterthought within the context of the overall sequence: women's liberation is here now and things in America are changing for women, even minority women. To give a complete picture of the changing world of the Río Grande Valley, Hinojosa needs to deal with this issue, but somehow *Becky* falls short. Hinojosa seems to be paying a kind of lip service to the idea of the independent woman. Perhaps it fails because there are so few Beckys in that part of the world. Perhaps he has tried to transfer successful women from academia to the Valley, but they do not move well. The novel is ostensibly about Becky and her decision to leave a marriage orchestrated by her mother to a man who is a toady for the powerful Anglo banker, Noddy Perkins. (Ironically, Perkins is also the employer of Jehú Malacara, whom Becky marries after her divorce.)

According to Lionel Villa, Elvira Caldwell, Becky's mother, expended a great deal of energy arranging the marriage between her daughter and Ira Escobar primarily because she wanted the family connection to the Leguizamón clan. So Becky's life is manipulated first by her own mother; after she is married, her life is run by her husband's employer, Noddy Perkins. Villa claims in the first interview in *Becky* that besides "politicking for her husband," Becky is used as "a prop, visible here and there, but a prop" (21). She is granted "unanimous membership" in all the local women's clubs and hobnobs with the social élite of Klail City. Finally, she realizes that it all has very little to do with her, but a lot to do with her husband's position. At some point shortly before her thirty-fifth birthday, she sees herself as a kept woman and as the tool of a nasty political and social system. According to her uncle, at that moment she sees that "having to depend on someone else for a living, to depend on someone else for anything, to be nothing but a kept-though-married woman was not the way to live. She saw what being independent meant" (23).

Hinojosa's insistence on the liberation of Becky Caldwell Escobar Malacara ultimately weakens the novel in that no proof exists that Becky really becomes independent, if it is even possible never "to depend on someone else for anything" (23). For one thing, she comes into an inheritance when she turns thirty-five. Even though the potency of this fact is diluted by her uncle's disclaimer that it's "not much" and that a trust has to be established for her children in order to keep the inheritance out of the community property settlement, Becky is also awarded in the divorce settlement the house she had shared with Ira and part of his pension. She does take a job with Viola Barragán, who "stepped in to help Becky, help her with a little boost, to make her independent. Her own person" (21). Viola does this so that Becky can be, as Villa says, "economically independent" (20). And then Becky marries Jehú. All of this suggests that any young, college-educated mother of two can become "her own person" if she has some money, a friend to offer her a challenging career, and perhaps a new husband, who is "a good man" with "a pair on him that clang when he walks" (17). Except for the emotional turmoil—and even that is downplayed as Becky rearranges her life with "no crying, no hiccups, no shortness of breath, and no raising of the voice" (22)—Becky seems to get on with it very nicely. For

Becky, things have a way of working out—to the point
of incredibility.

The idea of using a female character to depict
the changes of the last thirty years or so within the
Mexican-American community is a good one, or would
be if the character were believable. To have Becky
"cut loose from Ira" while simultaneously "cutting the
umbilical cord" from her mother is by now a fairly
standard variation on a theme—fiction written by
women has been dealing with this sort of thing for at
least two decades: Mary Gordon's *Final Payments*
(1978), with its Catholic undertones, is a good comparison, but by the seventeenth century at least this
was a concern of educated women. In a more contemporary setting, the late 1950s, Doris Lessing in "To
Room Nineteen" approaches the question of how
women can be their "own persons." Marilyn French's
The Women's Room is one of the best-known popular
fictions to tackle this subject, and Becky's concerns,
as we are "informed" of them, are very similar to those
of unnumbered other fictional heroines. In Becky's
case the umbilical cord leads directly back to her
mother, but in most feminist fiction, the umbilical cord
is truly symbolic, representing the restrictions (biological *and* social) on the female's attempts at personal freedom. Becky, however, is unlike most such
females in that she approaches her situation without

much soul-searching, untroubled by doubt, march-
ing blindly, it seems, into a new life.

   This is perhaps where Becky is revealed to be an
automaton of the author's creation rather than a believable or even particularly sympathetic character.
But Becky finally fails simply because she is not a
clearly delineated or realized character. As a tool of
the author, she does not have the strength to carry
the burden of symbol that he places on her. She remains a fuzzy outline. Alana Northcutt points out that
"the sharp-edged portrait of Becky painted in the letters of *Dear Rafe* is hard to reconcile with her new
image" (12). Hinojosa, however, puts Becky on a special plane. That she goes to work for Viola Barragán,
Hinojosa's prototype for the liberated woman, is made
to seem an earth-shattering event, but actually it is
hard to see the divorced Becky's motivation to work
as being much different from that of Inez Paredes's
in *Partners* or even the female bank tellers in ill-fit-
ting uniforms so pathetically described in the same
novel.

   The point is that it is hard to see what is supposed to be special about Becky, except that she is a
surrogate figure—she even repeats Hinojosa's exact
words as she tries to explain her new life: "Time's a
great leveller" (156). Much more than the character
of Police Lieutenant Rafe Buenrostro in *Partners*, or

the characters of Rafe and Jehú in the rest of the novels, she is more a vehicle than a character. She seems to exist primarily to allow Hinojosa a fictional representation of himself, and secondarily, to express what he perceives to be the views of the contemporary Mexican-American community on the issues of divorce and "women's liberation," issues that seem dated in the current economic climate.

In his effort to reclaim his sequence novel—after the aberration of *Partners in Crime*—Hinojosa takes up the female quest for a new identity, which is historically significant but may be out of his reach artistically. In *Becky*, he falls back on a fictional technique that served him well in such works as *Klail City*, *Claros Varones*, *Rites and Witnesses*, and the reportage section of *Dear Rafe*. In fact, *Becky* most resembles in form the second section of *Dear Rafe*, the one in which all the speculation about Jehú's absconding from the bank and from Klail City by various members of the community takes place. But by the time of the interviews in *Becky*, the much-respected P. Galindo is dead, and the interviewer in this novel remains enigmatic and unnamed, identified only as "the listener," a nephew of Lucas Barrón (*el Chorreao*). What Hinojosa hopes to achieve by the omission of name and personality in this case is not clear, though he most likely is trying to keep any element of didacticism out of the vignettes. He curiously fails to do so, and ultimately the commentary is more about the community than about Becky and what she is really like. And Becky herself is allowed not quite six pages in which to explain herself, even though the narrator says she "should speak for herself" (155).

This sort of diffuse treatment of the community as a whole is similar to what Hinojosa does in *The Valley*, but here there is no real drama. Not even the interest of past action is recalled. Most of the information about particular characters has appeared elsewhere, in some form or another, or else the interviewee just talks about himself, as in the case of Emilio Tamez, as he recounts his version of the breakup of his own marriage. This is not to say that some interesting summing up of the community, its past, present, and future, does not occur in *Becky*, but using Becky as a sort of catalyst for this dialogue of social history is ineffective as a dramatic device. As a novel, the work falls flat.

Though time has passed and conditions in the Valley *have* changed for the Mexican American as well as the Anglo, things are not as rosy as Hinojosa would have them seem in *Partners in Crime* and *Becky*. Also, these works make it seem that once the race struggle is settled, as it appears to be for these upwardly mobile characters at least, the *mejicano* is not a particularly interesting character. Most likely Hinojosa does not intend to create this effect, but he does, probably because he has now lost the emotional wellspring of his work. At this point in his own life, Hinojosa surely has a much harder time identifying with the average, non-university-educated Mexicanos than with mainstream Americans. As Charles Tatum says, Rafe and Jehú "have left their moorings in the Mexican community to become professionals. . . . They move comfortably in and out of the world dominated by Anglo capital and political power" (470). As Hinojosa personally achieved resolution to his own struggle, he no longer had a significant subject and was so far removed from the life of the Valley that he was no longer able to depict the full diversity of the contemporary community. This ultimately is the failure of the *Klail City Death Trip Series* as a work of fiction. The sense of urgency and dramatic intensity dies as the edge is taken off his main characters. Rafe is almost unrecognizable, and Jehú is practically invisible.

Once Hinojosa no longer feels the tension and conflict caused by the struggle to prove himself, the novels themselves are marred by a lack of tension and conflict—and ultimately a lack of control and purpose. In the novels set before the seventies Hinojosa seems to have a clearer sense of his artistic aims and firmer control of his fiction. It may be that memory has refined experience in these novels, making it more coherent and meaningful. In *Partners* and

Becky, he obviously sees the march of time and progress and attempts to delineate its ramifications for the world he knew as a child and young man, but these novels lack the depth of emotion of those early works, particularly *The Valley* and *Klail City*. It may be that history itself has robbed Hinojosa of his subject. As his own life and career progresses within the bureaucracy of the American university system, the ethnic flavor of his work fades. As his personal quest to forge a new identity comes to a successful end, the dramatic tension of the series is dissipated. Relying heavily on autobiography may add something to a fiction, but for Hinojosa, using his own experience and history as the cornerstone of his work finally proves that despite his excellences, he is unable to do with his life what James Joyce did.

Hinojosa is at his best when depicting the life of the Texas Valley from the 1930s through the 1950s or 1960s, but in this most recent period, he seems to be at a distance from the community. *Partners* could be set anywhere that a drug racket might flourish, and in *Becky*, the people who discuss her with the anonymous narrator treat the narrator like an outsider, a guest, rather than one of them. Nothing could be more substantively different from P. Galindo's interviews about Jehú at the end of *Dear Rafe*, in spite of the similarity of form. Most significant is the fact that Rafe and Jehú do not seem truly representative of the contemporary Mexican-American community, a fact in keeping with the autobiographical nature of these characters, but, in addition, in *Partners* and even in *Becky* the Mexican-American *community* is mostly absent. A few voices supplant the many.

The stories of the old timers are gone, and one might think that the *mejicano* in the Río Grande Valley has entered a brave new world, where the past is either forgotten or suppressed. For a sequence that overall is so concerned (as Hinojosa has said) to stick to the facts, to be honest and truthful, these two works do not give a complete picture of contemporary life in the Valley. If, however, the sequence is essentially autobiographical, then Hinojosa is being true and honest in showing the upscale, contemporary sort of lives Jehú, Rafe, and Becky are enjoying in the Texas Valley of the seventies and eighties. When an Anglo colleague invites Jehú over for a beer, Jehú responds by saying, "I'll bring some Riesling," to which the friend answers, "Riesling? Now you're talking. See you sevenish, buddy" (*Partners* 58).

For whatever reason, there is a lack of intimacy between the author and his material in *Partners in Crime* and *Becky and Her Friends*. Hinojosa places his characters in the Valley, but he is not there. Hinojosa has said that he wished to give an account of the Valley that he knows, and he seems to be on firm ground in all but these two novels. The distinctive regional flavor of works such as *The Valley*, *Klail City*, and *Rites and Witnesses* is absent from *Partners* and *Becky*. Their concerns are not uniquely connected to the life of the Río Grande Valley of Texas. Hinojosa tries to sustain a regionalist atmosphere in *Partners* by shattering Peter Hauer's misconceptions about Mexico and Mexicans, among other things, but this effort is a poor substitute for the vivid picture of the daily life of a community that is found in the earlier books.

Partners in Crime is really the more ambitious of the two works, and examining its weaknesses reveals the collapse of Hinojosa's fictional world as well as the failure of the novel itself as an example of genre fiction. The Rafe of *Partners* is not recognizable as the Rafe who went to the North Ward public school and endured the racial discrimination of Anglo teachers. Nor is he recognizable as the Rafe who recounts standing in a cantina listening to Echevarría tell the story of his father's death. Nor does he seem to have any significant scars from the horrific experience detailed earlier in *Korean Love Songs* and *The Useless Servants*.

If Hinojosa had not created a couple of convenient scenes in *Partners* to remind us of Rafe's tour of duty during the Korean War, we might easily forget that earlier youthful angst, bravado, and sensitivity, so cheerful and well-adjusted is this new Rafe. Rafe's

reaction to the gory sight of the men shot to pieces at
the Kum-Bak Bar is that of someone who has had to
get used to such things—and we know Rafe learned
to do so in Korea because a few chapters earlier, as
Rafe remembers the death of his wife, he recalls
briefly "what the dying had been like in Korea" (110).
When he sees how upset Irene Paredes is at the scene
of the crime, he tells her that it is possible to get used
to such things (120), but later thinks to himself that
she will never be able *entirely* to forget "a fingernail
attached to an index finger floating in a schooner of
red beer," something Rafe knows "from hands-on
experience" (193–94).

This Rafe is pretty hard-boiled when it comes to
blood and guts, but otherwise he is the stereotypical
detective and the practical but understanding lover
of Sammie Jo Perkins, who is married to the homosexual Sidney. The enigmatic and elusive Rafe who
receives Jehú's epistles in *Dear Rafe* now seems entirely accessible. In spite of any peculiarities—a certain secrecy about his private life, for example—Rafe
is a stock character in a mystery novel. The anger
that he may have felt as a *mejicano* boy and the trials of his young manhood have ostensibly been tempered by time and the evolving attitudes of Valley
Anglos and Mexican Americans.

The subtitle alone of *Partners* throws off the order and chronology of the *Death Trip* sequence. Call-

ing it "a Rafe Buenrostro Mystery" suggests that others have already been written and that still more are to follow. No further adventures of Rafe Buenrostro have followed, but Hinojosa has said that there will be a second mystery in the series (José David Saldívar, "Our Southwest" 183). If *Partners* were the first Hinojosa novel a reader were to encounter, he would think he was discovering a sequence of mystery novels. He would also be confused if he previously had read *Mi querido Rafa* rather than *Dear Rafe* because when Hinojosa reworked *Mi querido Rafa* as *Dear Rafe*, he added to the Preface the information that when Rafe was in William Barrett Veterans Hospital, he was already a non-practicing attorney and a lieutenant of detectives in the District Attorney's office in Belken County. This is never explained in any of the novels, but in *Partners in Crime*—also published in 1985—Rafe is once again depicted as an attorney and a detective. Hinojosa thus skews the pattern of the *Death Trip* sequence as far as form is concerned, just as Rafe's new demeanor skews the pattern of character development in the earlier works. Rafe goes from being a major character in a serious sequence novel to being a figure in a detective fiction that purports to be one of many.

Rafe is a figure of some distinction in *Partners*. He is the main character, and he is patterned after the superior detectives of any number of murder

mystery sequences: he is somehow extraordinary. He
is like Hillerman's shaman Jim Chee, P. D. James's
poet Detective Chief Inspector Adam Dalgliesh, Dorothy Sayers's intellectual marvel Lord Peter Wimsey,
or Agatha Christie's eccentric genius Hercule Poirot.
Though Rafe is not superstitious or openly religious
like Chee, though he is only a poet at heart and not
literally like Dalgliesh, though he must rely on pro-
cedure and hard work to solve cases and not on a
miraculous innate intuition like Wimsey, though he
is an "ordinary guy" rather than an eccentric like
Poirot, he is clearly cast in the tradition of these re-
nowned detectives, rather than in the hard-boiled
tradition of Raymond Chandler. Rafe is somewhat
genteel.

Rafe and his kind are élites among their colleagues, and they are usually shown to their best
advantage by the unwitting observations of lesser
mortals. In Rafe's case, this revelation comes in a
rather stilted conversation with young detective Peter Hauer. Rafe reveals that he is a literate, well-read,
well-rounded man by defending his friend Sam
Dorson when Hauer suggests that Dorson's gruff
manner might be caused by his jealousy of those on
the force, himself included, who have college degrees.
Peter's degree is from Trinity University in San Antonio (where Hinojosa taught from 1968 to 1970), but
when Rafe tells him that Sam has a degree from

Northwestern, "a good school," Peter does not know in which state it is located. When Rafe tells him it is in Evanston, by the lake, Peter reveals his ignorance once again by asking, "What lake?" (86). And it gets worse. The more uninformed Peter appears, the better Rafe looks. Though Rafe is defending Sam Dorson, it is clearly Hinojosa's intent to show the superiority of Rafe Buenrostro.

The truly revealing part of the dialogue is worth repeating: Rafe says that Sam "reads history," "likes music," and "reads *The New York Times*." Sam also "knows about plays, but he prefers operettas." Sam "quotes poetry," and, Rafe says, he "reads Housman, Hardy, Synge." Peter, of course, asks, "Who are they"? (86). Rafe, who attended another "good school," the University of Texas at Austin, just laughs. Here Hinojosa comes close to what Henry James called "the platitude of statement" (Blackmur xi). Even though an omniscient narrator does not reveal these facts about Sam Dorson's education, this contrived and artificial-sounding dialogue is not "representational" in the sense that James uses the term: one is aware that Hinojosa, the artist behind the scenes, is commenting not only about the tendency to stereotype policemen, but more important, that he is making an obvious statement about Rafe Buenrostro's tastes and intellect, and taking a shot at what he sees as the not-so-good schools in Texas.

James believed that "in art what is merely stated is not presented, what is not presented is not vivid, what is not vivid is not represented, and what is not represented is not art" (Blackmur xi). Perhaps to demand Jamesian skill and technique in a detective fiction is absurd, but the fact remains that in most of the earlier novels, Hinojosa achieves "representation" most of the time. In this particular scene between Rafe and Peter Hauer, Hinojosa might have foregone the banal dialogue in which Rafe really comes off looking like a snob. This exchange between Rafe and Peter is more akin to what Virginia Woolf called "the dreary business of getting from lunch to dinner" than it is to the vivid representations of life in *The Valley*, *Klail City*, *Rites and Witnesses*, and others.

But Hinojosa is following a cliché of the genre. The young Peter Hauer is a slightly dim, or at least misguided, rookie who must be watched. He is also something of a prude, wincing at normal manly cursing and a teenager's admission that he "shot the finger" at a reckless driver (147). Hauer must also be given his comeuppance, and if it does not come naturally, then it must be arranged. Hauer, continually referred to as "Young Mr. Hauer," is sent on various missions designed to humble him. For example, Chapter Nineteen is entitled, "Captain Lisandro Gómez Solís and a day in the life of young Mr. Hauer." Hauer is sent to Barrones to pick up some copies of fingerprints and a photograph. As Sam Dorson says, "He can pick up some education and no small amount of humility while he's there" (133). Hauer's earlier questioning of Rafe about Sam Dorson's education has clearly been discussed with Solís. When Hauer arrives in Solís's office, he is disconcerted by Solís's apparent ability to read his mind, but he is left nearly speechless when Solís pushes his framed university diploma from the University of Illinois (the institution which awarded a Ph.D in Spanish to Hinojosa) across the desk to Hauer. Hinojosa's intention here is clear—to make a statement about American perceptions of the Mexican, and to set Hauer up once again as a foil to the wise men, particularly Rafe, Dorson, and Solís.

The failure of the plot of *Partners in Crime* is in many ways caused by Hinojosa's attempt to fit in all of the clichés of the contemporary murder mystery, which is as much a novel of manners as anything else. Hinojosa attempted a kind of novel of manners in *Rites and Witnesses*, and there he was more successful because he was not imitative, as he is in *Partners*. And of course, since Rafe is the main character, many of the clichés—like that of the superior detective—revolve around him. The superior detective often has a painful past of some sort. Adam Dalgliesh's wife and young son were killed in an automobile crash. Rafe Buenrostro lost his young wife, Conchita, by drowning. Lord Peter Wimsey suffered shellshock in World War I. Rafe Buenrostro saw action in the Korean War. Even Hercule Poirot has known hardship as a Belgian refugee. Living in England proves to be a trial, and Poirot is always referred to as a "foreign" gentleman. Rafe—at least in the earlier novels—has known what it means to be an outsider.

The superior male detective, though he may be attractive to women, usually lacks a wife and is in no hurry to find one. (He is similar to the cowboy figure in this regard.) Again, Adam Dalgliesh and Hercule Poirot are good examples, though there are many others. Those detectives who do have wives are generally—like Rafe—police detectives, who cannot easily team up with their wives to solve mysteries. Having lost his wife of one year, Rafe is now involved with a married woman; their relationship is never developed beyond the obligatory, but tasteful, sexual encounters. It seems unlikely that Rafe and Sammie Jo will ever settle down to the predictable routine of married life. That she is married enables Rafe to remain free. That Sammie Jo's husband is a homosexual relieves Hinojosa from having to justify Rafe's involvement with her.

It has long been understood that the mystery novel is essentially moralistic in that right must triumph, and the superior detective is like a knight on a quest—seeking truth and good over evil. It would not do for such a detective to be a wife stealer or a womanizer in the James Bond tradition. Though Sammie Jo's husband Sidney's homosexuality is revealed in an earlier novel and is not created specifically for *Partners*, Hinojosa understands the benefit of using Sammie Jo as Rafe's lover rather than, say, having Rafe have an affair with the wife of Sam Dorson. If Rafe is to be effective as the hero of the type of mystery Hinojosa is trying to write, he must remain above moral censure, a fact that Hinojosa bows to again in the scene in which Gómez Solís reveals that his men—Mexican nationals—have made an arrest in Texas. Rafe says to his friend and colleague Solís, who is "building a case" for the Klail City detectives, "You realize we have to report the illegal arrest, don't you?" (186). No hard feelings result: Rafe is a man of integrity and Solís knows it. He knows when he mentions the arrest what Rafe's response will be.

Hinojosa has clearly abandoned many—if not most—of his earlier subjects and themes in this novel, subjects and themes that he fails to recapture in *Becky and Her Friends*. With the publication of these two works, Hinojosa's characters come to the end of their journey.

---

[1] See also Juan Bruce-Novoa's argument that *Partners* fits into the series in "Who's Killing Whom in Belken County."

[2] Becky's "Chicana consciousness" is offered as an explanation for the incongruity of *Becky* in the *Death Trip Series* by Bryce Milligan in "Plugging Away at the Truth."

[3] Serge Ricard says that the earlier ethnic divisions are now "toned down" and that the Valleyites are all "Texan" first who "discreetly" nurture their small differences" ("Drogue Sans Frontiére," 169–77).

[4] Hinojosa says Viola Barragán "seems to be the strongest woman character that I have," in José David Saldívar's "Our Southwest: An Interview with Rolando Hinojosa."

[5] Rafe, Dorson, and Solís exhibit some of the white man/dark man phenomenon that Leslie Fiedler describes in "Come Back to the Raft Ag'in, Huck Honey!" Though I fail to see any incipient homoerotic tendencies in this triangle, the relationship between Rafe and Dorson in particular is strangely reminiscent of that of Natty Bumpo and Chingachgook, Huck and Jim, and Ishmael and Queequeg, though the roles are not static.

7

Paradise Lost
and Found

In many ways, the novels
and poems of Rolando Hinojosa reflect the actuali-
ties of life for the *mejicano* in Texas, and his depiction of the segregation of the *barrios*, the second-class
citizenship, the enforced ethnicity, account for the regionalism in his *Death Trip*. As the historian Arnoldo
de Léon says, "Segregation in Texas and the rest of
the nation prolonged a Mexican ethnicity" for the
Mexican American. But de Léon goes on to demonstrate that although the repressive Anglo culture was
the primary cause of the separate status of the Mexican American, other factors within the Mexican-

American community were also at work. A strong link between Mexico and Mexican Americans existed well into this century, including the continued "activities of the Mexican consuls in Texas" during 1930–1945, newspapers from Mexico, and shared holidays such as *Cinco de Mayo* and *Diez y Seis de Septiembre*. Movie theaters in South Texas featured Mexican matinee idols. All of these facts, along with a shared language, helped to keep the Mexican American from recognizing the possibility of a different life (de León, *Mexican-Americans* 99).

Like de León, Rolando Hinojosa sees the multifaceted nature of the Mexican American's struggle for first-class citizenship. His *Death Trip Series* reveals both the insularity of the Mexican-American community and its yearning toward connections with the larger society. No stranger to racial discrimination, Hinojosa also understands the power of the familiar, comfortable ethnic identity. As he moves his narrative along from the world of the Texas Valley in the 1930s through the 1970s, he reveals the difficulty not only of moving forward through the slowly weakening walls of racial discrimination, but also of leaving behind much of what constituted a distinct ethnic identity. As a result, the *Klail City Death Trip Series* is shaped in large degree by the concepts of gain and loss, loss and compensation. In fact, the series as a whole argues for the inescapable fact that gain and loss are inseparable components not only of history, but also of every human life. Hinojosa's philosophical stance on this facet of human experience is the wise but practical position that one can only accept the inevitable with as much grace and humor as possible.

Despite a sometimes shattered chronology and unevenly developed characters, the series is driven by this sense of the inevitable. Hinojosa's characters are on a road that carries them to their destiny. While bypassing in large part the political activism of the 1960s and *El Movimiento*, Hinojosa moves his characters into the Anglo enclaves of law enforcement, banking, and business. In doing so, he represents only a small portion of the Mexican-American population: in 1970, sixty to seventy percent of Mexican-American male workers "functioned in unskilled and semiskilled occupations." Most were poor, especially the *campesinos*, whose children, like those of southern sharecroppers before them, had little chance of education (de Léon, *Mexican-Americans* 122–23). Yet it is hard to be overly critical of Hinojosa's failure to treat the full community in his later novels, although the early works do give a complete picture of a whole community. As the series progresses, Hinojosa turns his eye almost exclusively on the middle-class Mexican American. And of course by the time Hinojosa was writing in earnest in the mid-1970s, the radical-

ism of the Chicano movement had waned. As de Léon
says,

> In the end the changing times made the
> *movimiento* seem anachronistic. Its militant
> rhetoric and tactics seemed passé. Many of
> the Movement's aims became institutional-
> ized as well. (*Mexican-Americans* 132)

Along with this fact, another is perhaps even more
important to the focus of the *Death Trip Series*: "The
syncretization of cultures . . . has not produced a 'typical Tejano' nor is the 'world of Tejanos one of two cultural polarities'" (de Léon, *Mexican-Americans* 144).
Though Hinojosa himself and other Mexican-American academics have argued for the idea of a "cultural
polarity" or a cultural dialectic, de Léon says that a
large number of Tejanos have undergone an experience that "resembles the classic pattern of immigration accommodation" (*Mexican-Americans* 144). Even
without documented evidence, any reader of Hinojosa's *Death Trip Series* could discern these basic
truths about the Mexican-American community.
    So if Hinojosa does not appear especially radical
or overtly political, he nevertheless treats a significant element of the Mexican-American experience,
giving us insight into what may be only less dramatic
rather than less authentic. Felipe de Ortega y Gasca

says the Chicano writer must "praise the people, identify the enemy, and promote the revolution" (17).
Hinojosa, however, praises only some of the people—
and some of them are Anglo. He sees the enemy as he
truly is—often Anglo, but sometimes *mejicano*. The
revolution he promotes is primarily an education revolution—a revolution not of separatism, but of inclusion. He wants the Mexican American to join his
"enemy" as much as beat him. This point of view itself removes any potential element of pure radicalism from the *Death Trip Series*.

Lacking true revolution and radicalism, the
Death Trip Series ultimately reveals itself as yet another variation on the themes of the American frontier and the American Dream. Its significance in
American letters may rest as much on that fact as on
its depiction of a regional culture, for no matter how
diverse the body of American literature appears, each
of its components, each piece of its literature, must
come to terms with the same forces of myth: those
peculiarly American myths which for better or worse
have been so interrelated with American politics and
culture and even geography since the early days of
the Republic. Hinojosa acknowledges that this is the
truth when he says that

> Chicano literature . . . has its roots in Mexi-
> can literature, and Mexican-American writ-

ers have their roots in Mexico. . . . Roots, however, are not to be confused with the trunk of
the tree itself or with the branches that
spring from it. For, despite the Mexican in-
fluences, the Mexican-American writer lives
in and is deeply influenced by his life in the
United States. To date, the one prevalent
theme in Mexican-American writing is the
Chicano's life in his native land, the United
States. ("Mexican-American Literature" 423)

The intense relationship between American politics
and policy and American literature—both shapers and
reflectors of myth—is noted by critic Denis Donoghue
in *Reading America*:

The academic pursuit of themes in American Studies can't be neutral or disinterested.
You think you are talking about an American novel, but before you are well begun, you
find yourself reflecting on the exercise of
power in the world. This doesn't happen when
you talk about *Ulysses*. (4)

Donoghue calls America one of the few countries in
the world which had "a sense of a particular destiny"
from the beginning. Therefore, the "origin and its af-
termath must be peculiarly tense. . . . All it can do in

the meantime is live up to that destiny or renounce it" (5–6). Hinojosa's characters suffer from the necessity of living up to *and* renouncing their particular destinies, and in this they are connected to all fictional heroes who must choose one way of life over another. Of course, the American myth has many manifestations: the New Eden, the new world and new identity, the great democracy, the wilderness/ frontier, the aristocracy of worth, the aristocracy of wealth, and isolation and inclusion. The list goes on. Still the myth endures: it is sufficiently powerful to withstand myriad fragmentations. American literature and American minds are preoccupied with this myth, and no matter what their points of view, they cannot escape its existence or its force.

Hinojosa's *Death Trip* presents another perspective on American myth, a perspective that finally helps us to see Hinojosa as more "American" and less "Chicano." R. W. B. Lewis's observations on the American novelist express the dilemma in which Hinojosa and his characters find themselves:

> The solitary hero and the alien tribe; "the simple genuine self against the whole world"—this is still the given for the American novelist. The variable is this: the novelist's sense of the initial tension—whatever it is confronting, or whether it is poten-

> tially tragic; whether the tribe promises love,
> or whether it promises death. (111)

Hinojosa vacillates, and rightly so, for the journey
his characters make is potentially tragic—and yet
ultimately comforting; in a sense, the "alien tribe"
promises both love *and* death, love in the sense of a
kind of acceptance and security, but a death of the
old self. Still, despite such wrenching circumstances,
Hinojosa puts his faith in what Leslie Fiedler calls
the "chief effective religion" of modern America—op-
timism ("Novel and America" 135). Partly as a result
of this outlook, the series ultimately celebrates educational and material advantage over ethnic homo-
geneity. Hinojosa's acceptance of this phenomenon
may reflect his awareness of the perversion of the
American Dream; nevertheless, in twentieth-century
America, there is no alternative, except in a spiritual
sense. One cannot truly escape to the wilderness because there is no wilderness there. Neither can one
fight his way through the wilderness and enter a new
Eden, at least not literally; for Hinojosa's characters
the Anglo world stands as metaphor for the old American idea of "wilderness." For them, the Eden of economic, social, and political parity is at the same time
a wilderness composed of racial discrimination and
other more subtle psychological barriers. One cannot
simply stay put or retreat from this struggle because

another powerful component of American myth is also at work: the necessity of creating a new identity in a new world. As Wright Morris says of the American writer,

> The true territory ahead is what he must imagine for himself. He will recognize it by its strangeness, the lonely pilgrimage through which he attained it, and through the window of his fiction he will breathe the air of his brave new world. (365)

Each of these aspects of American myth contains its own dialectic. One strives both toward and against. As a consequence, the dramatic tension of the *Klail City Death Trip Series* comes from an elemental ambivalence about the loss of the old identity and the shaping of a new one. The often wrenching transformation of the minority into a being who is, for all practical purposes, one of the majority is the central issue for Rolando Hinojosa and his fictional world. All but the novels *Partners in Crime* and *Becky and Her Friends* depict a world that is either dead or dying; this is the world that Hinojosa and his characters have left behind, both literally and figuratively. It is only a memory, a sketch, a portrait. Yet we come to see that no alternative exists, and we cannot really fault Hinojosa for the new tempo of life found in

Partners and *Becky*. As Richard Howard has said of
James Wright,

> We must not succumb to the temptation of
> despising a poet's created world because he
> has desisted from it; indeed it is rather our
> obligation, when a convention has been ef-
> fected and another covenant vouchsafed, to
> trace connections, to show the Old Adam
> lurking about the confines of the New Jerusa-
> lem. (567)

In the end, the *Death Trip* is optimistic, even oddly
romantic. Despite the awesome barriers, Hinojosa's
heroes make it to the other side. A change in psycho-
social-political-economic geography creates a new
world and a new identity. This change is peculiarly
American, brought on by what seems at times the
almost demonic character of democracy, as it is described by Henry James, Sr., in a quotation R. W. B.
Lewis uses as epigraph to a chapter of *The American
Adam* entitled "The Case Against the Past":

> Democracy . . . is revolutionary, not forma-
> tive. It is born of denial. It comes into exist-
> ence in the way of denying established
> institutions. Its office is rather to destroy the

old works, than fully to reveal the new. (Lewis 13)

The painfulness and the enduring sense of loss engendered by such a "revolution" is made evident by the *Klail City Death Trip Series*, and yet the irony of Hinojosa's title becomes double-edged by the end of the series, with as much emphasis on the destination as on what is left behind. What is newly created stands in opposition to what has been destroyed. Yet Hinojosa seems eager to agree with Wordsworth that in spite of what is lost, "Other gifts / Have followed; for such loss, I would believe / Abundant recompense."

Works Cited

PRIMARY SOURCES

BOOKS

Becky and Her Friends. Houston: Arte Público, 1990.

Claros Varones de Belken. Trans. Julia Cruz. Tempe, AZ: Bilingual, 1986.

Dear Rafe. Houston: Arte Público, 1985.

Estampas del valle y otras obras. Trans. Gustave Valadez and José Reyna. Berkeley: Editorial Justa, 1973.

Generaciones y Semblanzas. Trans. Rosaura Sánchez. Berkeley: Justa Publications, 1987.

Klail City. Houston: Arte Público, 1987.

Korean Love Songs. Berkeley: Justa Publications, 1978.

Partners in Crime. Houston: Arte Público, 1985.

Rites and Witnesses. Houston: Arte Público, 1982.

The Useless Servants. Houston: Arte Público, 1993.

The Valley. Ypsilanti, MI: Bilingual, 1983.

ARTICLES

"Chicano Literature: An American Literature with a Difference." *The Rolando Hinojosa Reader*. Ed. José David Saldívar. Houston: Arte Público, 1985. 39–43.

"*La Prensa*: A Lifelong Influence of Hispanics in Texas." *Américas Review* 17 (Fall-Winter) 3–4, 125–29.

"Mexican-American Literature: Toward an Identification." *Books Abroad* 49 (1975): 422–30.

"The Sense of Place." *The Rolando Hinojosa Reader*. Ed. José David Saldívar. Houston: Arte Público, 1985. 18–24.

"The Texas-Mexico Border: This Writer's Sense of Place." *Open Spaces, City Places: Contemporary Writers on the Changing Southwest*. Ed. Judy Nolte Temple. Tucson: U of Arizona P, 1994. 95–101.

"This Writer's Sense of Place." *The Texas Literary Tradition: Fiction, Folklore, History*. Ed. Don Graham, James W. Lee, William T. Pilkington. Austin: UT College of Liberal Arts and the Texas State Historical Association, 1983. 120–24.

"Tomás Rivera (1935–1984)." *Tomás Rivera 1935–1984: The Man and His Work*. Ed. Rolando Hinojosa, Vernon E. Lattin, and Gary D. Keller. Tempe, AZ: Bilingual Review, 1988. 64–65.

"A Voice of One's Own." *The Rolando Hinojosa Reader*. Ed. José David Saldívar. Houston: Arte Público, 1985. 11–17.

SECONDARY WORKS

Adler, Jerry, and Tim Padgett. "Selena Country." *Newsweek* 23 October 1995: 76.

Agrella, Catherine. Rev. of *Becky and Her Friends*, by Rolando Hinojosa. *Dallas Morning News* 25 November 1990: J7.

Allsup, Carl. *The American GI Forum: Origins and Evolution*. The Mexican American Monograph Series. Austin: Center for Mexican American Studies, 1982.

Alurista. "Cultural Nationalism and Chicano Literature." *Missions in Conflict: Essays on U.S.-Mexican Relations and Chicano Culture*. Ed. Renate von Bardeleben, Dietrich Briesemeister, and Juan Bruce-Novoa. Tübingen: Gunter, Narr Verlage, 1986. 41–52.

Anaya, Rudolpho. "A Chicano in King Arthur's Court." *Old Southwest / New Southwest: Essays on a Region and its Literature*. Ed. Judy Lensink. Tucson: Tucson Public Library, 1987. 113–18.

Arnold, Matthew. "Stanzas from the Grand Chartreuse." *The Norton Anthology of English Literature*, Fifth Edition, v. 2. Ed. M. H. Abrams. New York: W. W. Norton and Company, 1962. 1383.

Bakhtin, Mikhail Mikhailovich. *The Dialogic Imagination*. Trans. Caryl Emerson and Michael Holquist. Austin: U Texas P, 1981.

Banta, George. Preface. *Texas' Last Frontier: A Brief History of the Lower Rio Grande Valley*. By Frank Pierce. Menasha, WI: George Banta, 1917. n. pag.

Blackmur, Richard P. Introduction. *The Art of the Novel* (1907). By Henry James. New York: Scribner's, 1980. vii–xxxix.

Bowden, Edwin T. *The Dungeon of the Heart: Human Isolation and the American Novel*. New York: Macmillan, 1961.

Boyd, Michael. *The Reflexive Novel: Fiction as Critique*. London: Associated UP, Inc., 1983.

Bruce-Novoa, Juan. "Chicanos in Mexican Literature." *Missions in Conflict: Essays on U.S.-Mexican Relations and Chicano Culture*. Ed. Renate von Bardeleben, Dietrich Briesemeister, Juan Bruce-Novoa. Tübingen: Gunter, Narr, Verlage, 1986. 55–64.

———. "Cultural Identity and Language in Mexico and Texas." *The Texas Journal of History, Ideas and Culture* 9.2 (Spring, 1987): 25.

———. "Rolando Hinojosa." *Chicano Authors: Inquiry by Interview*. Austin: U Texas P, 1980. 49–65.

———. "Who's Killing Whom in Belken County." *Revista monográfica* 3:1–2 (1987): 288–97.

Bus, Heiner. "The Establishment of Community in Zora Neale Hurston's *The Eatonville Anthology* (1926) and Rolando Hinojosa's *Estampas del valle* (1973)." *European Perspectives on Hispanic Literature of the United States*. Ed. Genevieve Fabre. Houston: Arte Público, 1988. 66–81.

Busby, Mark. "Faulknerian Elements in Rolando Hinojosa's *The Valley*." *MELUS* 11.4 (1984): 103–109.

— — —. "The Significance of the Frontier in Contemporary American Fiction." *The Frontier Experience and the American Dream: Essays on American Literature*. Ed. David Mogen, Mark Busby, and Paul Bryant. College Station: Texas A&M UP, 1989. 95–103.

Calderón, Héctor. "Texas Border Literature: Cultural Transformations and Historical Reflections in the Works of Américo Paredes, Rolando Hinojosa, and Gloria Anzaldúa." *Dispositio* 16.41 (1991): 13–27.

Calderón, Hector, and José David Saldívar, Ed. *Criticism in the Borderlands: Studies in Chicano Literature, Culture, and Ideology*. Durham: Duke UP, 1991.

Carranza, Eliu. *Pensamientos on Los Chicanos: A Cultural Revolution*. Berkeley: California Book Company, Ltd., 1969.

Chipman, Donald. *Spanish Texas: 1519–1821*. Austin: U Texas P, 1992.

Cisnéros, Sandra. Interview. "A Rough Start: Writer Sandra Cisnéros Recalls Hard Times in Austin," by Anne Morris. *Austin American Statesman* 17 Sept. 1993: C1.

Cota-Cárdenas, Margarita. "*Mi querido Rafa* and Irony: A Structural Study." *The Rolando Hinojosa Reader*. Ed. José David Saldívar. Houston: Arte Público, 1985. 158–69.

Dasenbrock, Reed. "An Interview with Rolando Hinojosa." *Translation Review* 27 (1988): 3–8.

de León, Arnoldo. "Cultural Identity and Language in Mexico and Texas." *The Journal of History, Ideas and Culture* 9.2 (1987): 25.

— — —. *Mexican-Americans in Texas: A Brief History*. Arlington Heights, IL: Harlan Davidson, 1993.

— — —. *They Called Them Greasers: Anglo Attitudes Toward Mexicans in Texas, 1821–1900*. Austin: U Texas P, 1983.

de los Santos, Alfredo G. "Facing the Facts about Mexican America." *Tomás Rivera 1935–1984: The Man and His Work*. Ed. Rolando Hinojosa, Vernon E. Lattin, and Gary D. Keller. Tempe, AZ: Bilingual Review, 1988. 113–19.

de Ortega y Gasca, Felipe. "Shaping the Canon." Unpublished essay, 1990.

de Tocqueville, Alexis. "Of Individualism in Democratic Countries." *Democracy in America* (Henry Reeve text). v.2. New York: Random House, 1945. 104–106.

Donoghue, Denis. *Reading America: Essays on American Literature*. New York: Knopf, 1987.

Dubose, Louis. "Rolando Hinojosa's Valley of Politics." Rev. of *Dear Rafe*, by Rolando Hinojosa. *The Texas Observer* 8 Nov. 1985: 15–16.

Espinosa, Susan. "Valley Sleuthing." Rev. of *Partners in Crime*, by Rolando Hinojosa. *The McAllen Monitor* 2 Feb. 1986: C11.

Fiedler, Leslie. "Come Back to the Raft Ag'in, Huck Honey!" *An End to Innocence: Essays on Culture and Politics*. Boston: Beacon, 1948. 142–51.

— — —. "The Novel and America." *A Fiedler Reader*. New York: Stein and Day, 1977. 131–46.

García, Ed. "¿Quién es Rolando Hinojosa?" *The Texas Observer* 11 March 1983: 26–27.

García, Mario T. Interview. "A Lasting Pride: Academics, Participants Consider Victories, Historical Meaning of Chicano Movement," by Frank Trejo. *Dallas Morning News* 19 Sept. 1993: A1, p. 20.

Gonzalez-Berry, Erlinda. "*Estampas del Valle*: From Costumbrismo to Self-Reflecting Literature." *The Bilingual Review / La Revista Bilingue* 7:1 (Jan.-Apr.) 28–29.

Gonzalez-Gerth, Miguel. "Borgas and Texas: Farewell to an Old Friend." *Vortex* 112 (1987): 1, 13–15.

Hardwick, Elizabeth. *Seduction and Betrayal: Women in Litera-
    ture*. New York: Random House, 1974.

Howard, Richard. "James Wright: 'The Body Wakes to Burial.'"
    *Alone with America: Essays on the Art of Poetry in the United
    States since 1950*. New York: Athenaeum, 1971. 575–86.

Johnston, Jill. "Fiction of the Self in the Making." *New York Times
    Book Review* 25 April 1993: 29.

Karolides, Nicholas J. *The Pioneer in the American Novel: 1900–
    1950*. Norman: U of Oklahoma P, 1964.

Kearney, Milo and Anthony Knopp. *Border Cuates: A History of
    the U.S.-Mexican Twin Cities*. Austin: Eakin, 1995.

Kellman, Steven G. *The Self-Begetting Novel*. New York: Colum-
    bia UP, 1980.

Leal, Luis. "History and Memory in *Estampas del valle*." *The
    Rolando Hinojosa Reader*. Ed. José David Saldívar. Houston:
    Arte Público, 1985. 101–108.

— — —. "Mexican-American Literature: A Historical Perspective."
    Modern Chicano Writers. Ed. Joseph Sommers and Tomás
    Ybarra-Fausto. Englewood Cliffs, NJ: Prentice-Hall, 1979.
    18–30.

León-Portilla, Miguel. "Cultural Identity and Language in Mexico
    and Texas." *Texas Journal of History, Ideas and Culture* 9.2
    (1987): 25.

Lewis, R. W. B. *The American Adam*. Chicago: U of Chicago P,
    1955.

Limón, José. "Cultural Identity and Language in Mexico and Texas."
    Texas Journal of History, Ideas and Culture 9.2 (1987): 25.

McClain, Lawrence Lee. "The Rhetoric of Regional Identity: The
    Politics of American Literary History." Diss. U Texas at Aus-
    tin, 1993.

Martín-Rodríguez, Manuel M. "El Tema Ya Culpa En Cuatro
    Novelistas Chicanos." *The Hispanic Journal* 10.1 (Fall 1988):
    133–42.

———. "*Klail City Death Trip* de Rolando Hinojosa: La novela del lector." Diss. U California, Santa Barbara, 1991.

Mejía, Jaime Armin. "Breaking the Silence: The Missing Pages in Rolando Hinojosa's *The Useless Servants*." *Southwestern American Literature* 15.1 (1994): 1–6.

———. Rev. of *The Useless Servants*, by Rolando Hinojosa. *Southwestern American Literature* 18.2 (1993) : 96–97.

———. "Transformations in Rolando Hinojosa's *Klail City Death Trip Series*." Diss. Ohio State U, 1993.

Meyer, Michael C. and William L. Sherman. *The Course of Mexican History*. 3rd ed. Oxford: Oxford UP, 1987.

Milligan, Bryce. "Plugging Away at the Truth." *The Texas Observer* 28 September 1990: 28.

Montenegro, Marilyn. *Chicano and Mexican Americans: Ethnic Self-Identification and Attitudinal Differences*. San Francisco: R & E Research Associates, 1976.

Morris, Robert K. *Continuance and Change: The Contemporary British Novel Sequence*. Carbondale: Southern Illinois UP, 1972.

Morris, Wright. "The Territory Ahead." *Modern American Fiction: Essays in Criticism*. Ed. A. Walton Litz. New York: Oxford UP, 1963. 338–65.

Neate, Wilson. "The Function of Belken County in the Fiction of Rolando Hinojosa: The Voicing of the Chicano Experience." *American Review: A Review of Hispanic Literature and Art of the USA* 18:1 (Spring 1990): 92–102.

Northcutt, Alana. "Latest *Klail City* Novel Disappoints." Rev. of *Becky and Her Friends*, by Rolando Hinojosa. *Texas Books in Review* 10.4 (1990): 12.

Paredes, Américo. "The Folk Base of Chicano Literature." *Modern Chicano Writers*. Ed. Joseph Sommers and Tomás Ybarra-Frausto. Englewood Cliffs, NJ: Prentice-Hall, 1979. 4–17.

———. "Nearby Places and Strange-Sounding Names." *The Texas Literary Tradition: Fiction, Folklore, History*. Ed. Don Graham, James W. Lee, William T. Pilkington. Austin: U Texas College of Liberal Arts and the Texas State Historical Association, 1983. 130–38.

Penzenstadler, Joan. "La frontera, Aztlán, el barrio: Frontiers in Chicano Literature." *The Frontier Experience and the American Dream*. Ed. David Mogen, Mark Busby, and Paul Bryant. College Station: Texas A&M UP, 1989. 159–79.

Pierce, Frank C. *Texas' Last Frontier: A Brief History of the Lower Rio Grande Valley*. Menasha, WI: George Banta, 1917.

Randolph, Donald A. "Death's Aesthetic Proliferation in Works of Hinojosa." *Confluencia* 1.2 (1986): 38–47.

———. "Eroticism in War and the Eroticism of War in Hinojosa's *Korean Love Songs*." *Revista monográfica* 7 (1991): 218–26.

Reich, Alice Higman. *The Cultural Production of Ethnicity: Chicanos in the University*. Diss. U Colorado, 1980. Ann Arbor: UMI, 1982.

Ricard, Serge. "Drogue Sans Frontiere: Geographie D'Une Enquête Dans *Partners in Crime* de Rolando Hinojosa." *Multilinguisme et Multiculturalisme en Amérique du Nord: Espace seuils limites*. Ed. Jean Beranger and Jean Cazemajou. Talence, Bordeaux: Centre de Recherches sur l'Amerique Anglophone, Maison des Sciences de l'Homme d'Acquitaine, 1990. 169–77.

———. "An Interview with Rolando Hinojosa." *Revue francaise caiso d'etudes americaines*. 13:32 (1987): 193–96.

———. "Rolando Hinojosa: le bilinguisme tranquille du Mexican-Texan." *Ecritures Hispaniques aux Etats-Unis: Memoire et Mutations*. Ed. Yves-Charles Grandjeat. Aix-en-Provence: Universite de Provence, 1990. 139–66.

———. "Un Art de la Survie: Chicanismo et religion dans l'oeuvre de Rolando Hinojosa." Volume 7 of *Religion et Memorie ethnique au Canada et aux Etas-Unis. Le Facteur religieux en Amerique du Nord.* Eds. Jean Beranger and Pierre Guillaume. Talence, Bordeaux: Centre de Recherces sur l'Amerique Anglophone, Maison des Sciences de l'Homme d'Acquitaine, 1986. 325–41.

Riera, Miguel. "El Otro Sur: Entrevista con Rolando Hinojosa." *Quimera* 70/71 (1987): 112–17.

Rivera, Tomás. "Mexican-American Literature: The Establishment of a Community." *LA CHISPA.* Ed. Gilbert Paolini. New Orleans: Tulane UP, 1983. 231–39.

———. "Statement of Personal Outlook on the Future of American Higher Education." *Tomás Rivera 1935–1984: The Man and His Work.* Ed. Rolando Hinojosa, Vernon E. Lattin, and Gary D. Keller. Tempe, AZ: Bilingual Review, 1988. 52.

Rocard, Marciénne. "The Chicano: A Minority in Search of a Proper Literary Medium for Self-Affirmation." *Missions in Conflict: Essays on U.S.-Mexican Relations and Chicano Culture.* Ed. Renate von Bardeleben, Dietrich Briesemeister, Juan Bruce-Novoa. Tübingen: Gunter, Narr Verlage, 1986. 31–40.

"Rolando Hinojosa-Smith." *Contemporary Authors: Autobiography Series.* Detroit: Gale, 1992. 16:139–53.

Saldívar, José David. *The Dialectics of Our America: Genealogy, Cultural Critique and Literary History.* Durham: Duke UP, 1991.

———. "Our Southwest: An Interview with Rolando Hinojosa." *The Rolando Hinojosa Reader.* Ed. José David Saldívar. Houston: Arte Público, 1985. 180–90.

———. "Rolando Hinojosa's *Klail City Death Trip*: A Critical Introduction." *The Rolando Hinojosa Reader.* Ed. José David Saldívar. Houston: Arte Público, 1985. 44–63.

Saldívar, Ramón. *Chicano Narrative: The Dialectics of Difference.* U Wisconsin P, 1990.

— — —. "A Dialectic of Difference: Toward a Theory of the Chicano
    Novel." *Melus* 6:3 (1979): 73–92.

— — —. *"Korean Love Songs*: A Border Ballad and Its Heroes."
    The Rolando Hinojosa Reader. Ed. José David Saldívar. Hous-
    ton: Arte Público, 1985. 143–57.

Sánchez, Rosaura. "From Heterogeneity to Contradiction:
    Hinojosa's Novel." *The Rolando Hinojosa Reader*. Ed. José
    David Saldívar. Houston: Arte Público, 1985. 76–100.

Saroyan, William. *My Name Is Aram*. New York: Harcourt, Brace,
    1940.

Scholz, Lásló. "Fragmentarismo en *Klail City* y sus alredededores
    de Rolando Hinojosa." *Missions in Conflict: Essays on U.S.-
    Mexican Relations and Chicano Culture*. Ed. Renate von
    Bardeleben, Deitrich Briesemeister, and Juan Bruce-Novoa.
    Tübingen: Gunter, Narr, Verlage, 1986. 179–81.

Simmons, Ozzie G. *Anglo-Americans and Mexican-Americans
    in South Texas*. New York: Arno, 1974.

Sommers, Joseph. "Critical Approaches to Chicano Literature."
    Modern Chicano Writers. Ed. Joseph Sommers and Tomás
    Ybarra-Frausto. Englewood Cliffs, NJ: Prentice-Hall, 1979.
    31–40.

Spiller, Robert E., et al., eds. *Literary History of the United States*.
    3rd ed. London: Macmillan, 1963.

Tatum, Charles. "Review of *Partners in Crime: A Rafe Buenrostro
    Novel*." *World Literature Today* 60 (1986): 470.

Torres, Héctor. "Discourse and Plot in Rolando Hinojosa's *The
    Valley*." *Confluencia* 2.1 (1986): 84–93.

Trejo, Arnulfo D., ed. *The Chicanos: As We See Ourselves*. Tuc-
    son: U Arizona, 1979.

Index